The Joy of Imperfection

The Joy of Imperfection

Enid Howarth and Jan Tras

Fairview Press   *Minneapolis*

Published by Fairview Press, 2450 Riverside Avenue South, Minneapolis, MN 55454.

Library of Congress Cataloging-in-Publication Data

Howarth, Enid, 1934–
    The joy of imperfection / Enid Howarth and Jan Tras.
        p.   cm.
    ISBN 1-57749-011-8 (pbk. : alk. paper)
    1. Perfectionism (Personality trait) 2. Self-acceptance. 3. Individuality. I. Tras, Jan, 1943– . II. Title.
BF698.35.P47H68   1996
158'.1—dc20   96-19734
                                                                         CIP

First Printing: September 1996

Printed in the United States of America
00 99 98 97 96   7 6 5 4 3 2 1

Cover design: Barry Littmann
Author photo: Sam Howarth

Publisher's Note: Fairview Press publishes books and other materials related to the subjects of social and family issues. Its publications, including *The Joy of Imperfection,* do not necessarily reflect the philosophy of Fairview Hospital and Healthcare Services or their treatment programs.

For a free current catalog of Fairview Press titles, please call this toll-free number: 1-800-544-8207.

To dream of the person you would like to be
is to waste the person you are.
—*Unknown*

Contents

Introduction *ix*

1. Perfection, the Final Frontier? 1
2. I Can and Should Be Perfect? 7
3. Imperfection Equals Failure? 15
4. Something Is Wrong with Me? 25
5. True Love and Living Happily Ever After? 33
6. Father Knows Best? 43
7. Everyone Else Knows Best? 51
8. Mommy and Daddy Are to Blame? 59
9. Life Is Fair? 67
10. Original Guilt? 73
11. Codependents 'R' Us? 79
12. Controlling the Entire Universe? 89
13. Change Is Dangerous? 101
14. Silence Is Golden? 111
15. Happiness Is Hazardous? 119
16. I Am What I Achieve? 127
17. Never Too Rich or Too Thin? 137
18. Girls Are Made of Sugar and Spice? 151
19. Boys Are Made of Frogs and Snails? 161
20. Old Patterns Lead to New Results? 169
21. Do Everything Alone? 177
22. To Know Me Is to Leave Me? 183
23. The Perfect Relationship? 195
24. The Flip Side of Perfect 205
  Imperfection Poll *207*

Introduction

Commitment to perfection and the fear of failure are as American as motherhood and apple pie. When the American Dream says, "Be perfect," too often the American Experience is "I've failed—again." Ordinary citizens feel deeply flawed because they and their lives are less than perfect. Their jobs, parents, marriages, children, bodies, personalities, and selves are all disappointingly human. Cultural and inherited myths about perfection, buried so deep in our psyches that they seem to be simple reality, constrict us and make living and loving much harder than they need to be.

As good citizens, we felt it was our patriotic duty to write *The Joy of Imperfection,* to undermine our national addiction to perfection, and to remind our fellow Americans that being human is what we're really all about. As mental health counselors practicing in the wilds of New Mexico, we wrote this book for our clients, our families, our friends, and all those who punish themselves for being human and carry the shame of being imperfect.

The Joy of Imperfection focuses on the serious business of living happily. It's intended as a practical guide to console, inform, and delight. It challenges familiar icons and questions authority. It shines some light on fear, anger, denial, guilt, shame, and issues of self-esteem. It explores self-defeating belief systems, difficult relationships, and codependent behaviors. It speaks to anyone floating in an ocean of impossible dreams and expectations—students, parents, stressed professionals, baby boomers, codependents, twelve-steppers, type-A personalities—

anyone interested in personal growth, expanded awareness, or the humor in the human condition.

You don't have to be seriously distressed to enjoy this book. You do have to be willing to accentuate the positive, subvert the negative, laugh about the mess you're in, and admit that failure is its own reward. You can even share this book with a friend without implying that your friend is defective. We have kept it simple, kept it smart, kept it light. It's not penicillin, but more like a spring tonic, a vacation at the seaside, or a dozen roses.

The Joy of Imperfection began as "Perfect You're Not: The Adventure of Being Ordinary," a full-page article in the *Albuquerque Journal* on December 8, 1991. Readers wrote us letters telling us they'd saved it, laminated it, stuck it on their refrigerators. Parents sent it to their children. Teachers discussed it in class. Clearly, we had struck a resonating chord in the community. Surprised and delighted with these warm responses, we began to collaborate on a short, snappy expansion of our original article. Four intense and creative years later, we finished *The Joy of Imperfection*.

The book's insights into the human predicament come from our extensive experience with therapy, theater, and teaching. Enid has a Ph.D. in English literature and has been teaching at the University of New Mexico and counseling for nearly thirty years. She is a published poet, playwright, essayist, and critic. She does film reviews for public radio and is involved in local theater. Jan has an M.A. in counseling and works as a clinical counselor in both hospital settings and private practice. In her former life, Jan performed on Broadway and appeared in national television commercials. We are both licensed mental health counselors and collaborated as therapists and workshop facilitators before we began collaborating as writers.

Writing together has challenged all the common wisdom about how books are made. For us, it has been an unexpectedly exciting and synergistic process. We brainstormed sitting on the couch or in the backyard, drinking tea, eating cookies. We made notes and transformed them into ragged outlines, which we wrote on colored paper and pasted all over the office walls. Bits and pieces went into the computer, which became the container for our untidy, collective genius. Then we sat side by side in front of the screen and fussed over every sentence, word, and comma, birthing the mythical creature you now hold in your hands.

Introduction

Work had to stop as we taught ourselves how the computer made margins, paginated, and dropped bombs on innocent writers. We ignored our families. We neglected our dogs. Our houses were in chaos. We wrote and ate, wrote and laughed, wrote and wrote. And, still overflowing with great mutual respect and appreciation, we're still writing.

This book would not have been possible without the support of our families and friends. Special love to Peter, Nicholas, Rachel, Sam, Jo, and Anne. Many thanks to our last-minute hero, Sharon, our faithful publicist, Karen, our computer whiz, Skip, and the enthusiastic folks at Fairview.

1

Perfection, the Final Frontier?

Perfection, the final frontier—"to boldly go where no one has gone before," like Captain Kirk, Spock, Wonder Woman, Superman—is a grand illusion. Perfectionists long to be better than the best, to be flawless, to break world records, to bring home the gold again and again. Perfectionists dream of finding perfect solutions to the complex problems of the universe. What a challenge! What an illusion! What a way to make ourselves miserable!

Real people—not cartoon characters or made-for-TV members of the starship crew—never cross the final frontier between real life and the perfect life. Real people just can't get there from here. Real people have ups and downs, good days and bad, successes and failures, and, once in a while, a perfect moment. Sometimes we achieve a perfect tennis serve, a perfect soufflé, a perfect kiss. We remember those moments with great joy. We like to imagine we can have them always, or at least again and again. We can't. A moment is not a life. Life is zillions of moments—perfect, imperfect, ordinary, extraordinary, terrible, and wonderful. We can't have only the good moments, and we can't make any of them last forever. We can only allow exquisite moments to linger in our memories and provide us with pleasure and inspiration.

Most of us have spent years of our lives moving at warp speed toward some vision of the perfect self and the perfect life. We inherited

1

those visions from families, schools, books, movies, and TV—the world around us. Our most recent maps and tour guides were probably self-help articles, books, and tapes. Seeking perfection, we took a lot of advice. We tried to be positive and assertive, listen more actively, do pushups before breakfast, drink water before dinner, and take an aspirin before bed. We were encouraged to keep journals, record dreams, list assets, confront landlords, and repeat affirmations.

In pursuit of the perfect body, we might have decided to diet or not to diet, to try fruit juice fasts, or to eat brown rice and veggies or grapefruits and dry toast. We pumped iron, did yoga, race-walked, practiced T'ai Chi, or stair-stepped to heaven. How disappointed we were when we noticed that our genes had a lot to say about the shape and mass of our thighs, biceps, and belly. How depressed we were when we realized that the body we inherited was never going to look like the one we longed for. We all fought the losing battle with our DNA, tried to outsmart our cellular programming, and failed.

These struggles taught us a lot. Surely some of our efforts were helpful, but we still weren't perfect. We had some successes, but we always needed more work, more sweat, more changes, and more improvement. What looked like a straightforward path was really a not so merry-go-round, forever spinning, with no end in sight. The brass ring of perfection was always just out of reach. We could approach it, get really close, almost feel it in our grasp, just barely touch it. But it always eluded us. And these near catches kept us going. However, the painful truth is that we will not get to perfection from here. It may be time to step off the merry-go-round or climb out of the starship and feel the earth under our feet, to find a new brass ring or final frontier closer to home. It may be time to let ourselves rest.

The truth is, we are perfectly and uniquely imperfect—one of a kind, a very limited edition. Our imperfections enable us to be different, to explore new frontiers. To be flexible, imaginative, and creative. To have fun, to laugh, and to be ourselves.

Imagine living contentedly with your imperfect self, valuing your imperfect life, celebrating being adequate. Picture just being ordinary, enjoying being human, and feeling at home in the world. Imagine feeling really okay just the way you are and letting yourself relax. What a concept!

Totally unscientific experiments have made a major breakthrough, proving that recognizing and appreciating our imperfections can reduce stress, contribute to mental health, possibly cause weight loss (or gain), lower cholesterol count, deepen laugh lines, and of course enhance our sexuality. This is not a new concept but an ancient one. Navajo weavers have always believed that too much perfection is prideful and may offend the gods. They deliberately include a flaw in the beautifully symmetrical designs of their rugs, honoring human imperfection. Japanese flower arrangements deliberately use asymmetry to create unexpected forms and illusions, artificially heightening the natural beauty of the flowers. Borrowing ideas from these cultures can soften our American hardheadedness.

This culture we live in inherited its ideas about perfection from Plato, the ancient Greek genius who first described the notions of unattainable goals and impossible dreams. His ideas were translated by the church and transmitted to us through religion ("Strive for saintliness"), through schools ("Just work harder and you'll always get 100"), and at home ("If you'd only try, you could be our perfect child"). Authority figures often neglected to mention that the world is full of delicious possibilities and attainable goals. Imagine if we had been generously rewarded for enjoying school, coming in fourth, or being relaxed, comfortable, and satisfied.

This is not to knock excellence. Practice and dedication can indeed get us to Carnegie Hall, just like the New York cabdriver said. Even so, the performance only lasts two hours, the applause ten minutes, and the reviews one day. The only big payoff that lasts is love of the process—the day-after-day striving, hard work, and struggle. When we choose to put our time in, we can certainly accomplish great things. Still, although excellence is achievable, perfection is not.

We know this idea conflicts with messages we hear from people who make a lot of money telling us that perfection is indeed possible, desirable, and even necessary. They want us to believe that if we buy enough of their products or services, we too can be perfect. Consider the perfect model in the centerfold. No one tells us that she's spent hours and hours being made up, airbrushed, folded, spindled, pinched, and stapled into shape. We are encouraged to forget that no one real looks like her. Even she doesn't look like her. But women are told that if they buy the right clothes, makeup, and implants, they could maybe have the perfect body, man, bank account, and life. Men are told that if they buy the right clothes, car, and implants, they could maybe have the perfect body, woman, bank account, and life. So we dream and buy more, hoping the next purchase will get us there. Alas, it's all make-believe—an ad man's invention, a con man's story, a media hype, a sophisticated psychological ploy.

Make-believe has such great appeal. We all grew up on it. We played make-believe games and pretended they were real. Fairy tales promised more wonderful, more magical, more enchanted lives than the ones we were living. *Cinderella, Sleeping Beauty, Snow White, King Arthur, Robin Hood*, Hollywood movies, musicals, and TV taught us that our lives could be charmed. Men could be clever, brave, and strong enough to slay the dragon, defeat the enemy, and win the beautiful princess. Women could be forever young, gorgeous, and poised, waiting for the invincible handsome prince to rescue them. We could all ride off into the sunset and live happily ever after.

Sometimes we stay connected to myths and fairy tales because we remember our pleasure when we first heard them, the comfort of rainy afternoons in the library, the warmth of snuggling in front of the TV with a kid sister, or the security of being safely tucked in bed by one of our favorite grownups. We want to stay bonded to the storytellers, to our parents, friends, older brother, or Great-aunt Martha. Because we deeply cherish those remembered moments and long to maintain our sense of safety and permanence, we remain vulnerable to fairy tales. Those early images deep inside our memories and imaginations can keep us searching for the impossible life, keep us longing to be the impossible hero or the ideal princess, keep us dreaming the impossible dream.

The impossible dream has so much power that it can run our lives. It can grow to mythical proportions, like Jack's beanstalk or Paul Bunyan. It can lure us down a yellow brick road, toward an emerald green life in a technicolor Oz where nothing ever changes, all things happen for the best, and everyone stays forever young, strong, and joyful. What an addictive drama—seductive, irresistible, delusional, and so difficult to let go of.

But real life isn't Oz. It's more like Kansas. And we who live in the shifting and changing real world are forever creating and recreating our own life stories, editing and adding new characters and situations. Fortune, luck, fate, genes, and karma are our coauthors. We grow and change as life unfolds. Our stories are set in movable type. We're always writing new chapters based on new information. We make new choices because we know more now than we ever did. And so we change direction and remake old decisions. Life is not finished when an adventure is over. Amazing things do happen during " . . . happily ever after."

The part of us that cherishes the simple safety of childhood's fairy tales wants to believe that the world is an orderly and predictable place where good always triumphs over evil and wisdom prevails. But real life is as complicated as Kansas, and that's the truth. Living with this complexity is easier when we separate our present truths from the outdated tales we tell ourselves. We can move beyond smoke and mirrors, pull back the curtain, and see who the Wizard really is.

This is an excellent time of year to be fearless. Take the dog and leave Oz. Return home. Go to Kansas and live in the real world. With all its imperfections, ragged endings, and surprises, real life is alive with possibility. And you get to be the Wizard, the ordinary person who can create magic. You can throw the water of truth on the old illusions that keep you stuck, and melt the wicked myths of the West.

How do you do this? Be bold. Follow our yellow brick road to Kansas. Stop at those places that interest you. Race past those that don't. Stay with what you enjoy, and let the rest go by. Move at your own pace. Bon voyage!

Here's the road map to follow as you move along:
1. Each chapter will boldly name one cherished MYTH you might be ready (and happy) to leave behind.
2. Under each myth is a common-sense TRUTH that you probably already know but hate to admit. The TRUTH shouts, "Wake up! You're a fully flawed human. Your candidacy for sainthood has been denied." Carry this truth in your backpack to sustain you on your journey.
3. ONCE UPON A TIME offers helpful stories, fairy tales, and present-day anecdotes to spotlight sticky patches on the road.
4. IN THE BEGINNING describes some of the places where the myths originated, how they grew and flourished in the Petri dishes of our youth.
5. IN THE PRESENT is that little red arrow that says, "You are here." It shows how the myth continues to impact our adult psyches.

6. GOAL offers realistic alternatives to outdated beliefs, something to help you feel grounded on unfamiliar turf. It points toward a new destination.

7. STRETCH YOURSELF provides whimsical options and unexpectedly useful tactics to help you stay sane while germinating a new belief system. It offers strategies to keep you flexible and prevent you from being bored on the road less graveled.

8. AFFIRMATIONS are snacks to take along, irreverent messages to repeat when you need some nourishment. They're the goodies no one packed for you when you were growing up, so now you get to pack them for yourself.

Take a deep breath. Don't close your eyes. Here we go!

2

I Can and Should Be Perfect?

Myth

Perfection is attainable; therefore I can and should be perfect.
If I just do more, try more, learn more, work more, earn more,
buy more, exercise more, then I will be perfect.

Truth

No, you won't be perfect. You'll be tired, broke, stressed, sweaty, and feeling like a failure. Seeking the perfect face and body, the perfect partner, the perfect income, and the perfect life costs a lot of time, energy, and money. The cheap truth is that perfection is rare, fleeting, and usually accidental.

The hole in one, the game-winning grand slam, the gold-medal performance when every judge gives you a ten are rare and precious events in a lifetime. Even the greatest athletes, who spend their entire lives working toward perfection, know they might reach it for only a moment and then, inevitably, it will be gone. They never know if they will be lucky enough to reach it again. You, too, have had some perfect moments. But no matter how hard you try, perfect moments will remain elusive and unpredictable. You just can't hold onto them, or turn them into a perfect life or a perfect you.

In the beginning

Where did we get all these expectations? When we were small and vulnerable, grownups seemed giant, capable, and powerful, like gods. They defined our worlds. Their reactions shaped us and taught us who we were. We didn't invent ourselves. Initially, if grownups urged us to be better, we tried to be better. If they pushed us to be perfect, we tried to be perfect. When they were imperfect, and they were, we sometimes swore never to make their mistakes. We resolved to be more perfect than they were.

When we felt really loved and secure in our families, corrections were only information. When we felt unloved or insecure, corrections felt like criticism, rejection, threats, or attacks. We imagined there was something terribly wrong with us. We began to fear we'd lose the people we loved and needed if we didn't do things just right.

Once upon a time

A sweaty caveman came in from the hunt. He'd just cut up four hundred pounds of bison meat with a stone axe. He was tired and cranky. When he got back to his cave, there was no fire. His young son, happy to see his father, ran out to meet him and hear the story of the big kill. But the caveman was worn out and had no patience. He shouted at his son, scolding him for not building the fire. The boy cringed. "Damn," he might have said to himself in cave-ese, "I didn't do it right again. What's wrong with me? I've got to do better if I want my dad to love me and take me hunting." It's the same old story. For hundreds of generations, children have struggled to feel valued by tired, cranky, Neanderthal adults.

Children try to become perfect to gain love, affection, and praise. They try to avoid harsh looks, words of disappointment, scolding, shaming, or even the strap. When we were children, we may have felt pressured to be the perfect fire-builder, the perfect son or daughter, the perfect brother or sister. We may have been expected to be the perfect student, the perfect baseball player, or the perfect dishwasher. Neighbors, teachers, coaches, preachers, and people we don't even remember reinforced some of these messages. Their value judgments became part of us, the demanding voices we still hear in our heads. Echoes from childhood tell us we are flawed and have to keep trying to be better. We do to ourselves what the adult gods did to us when we were little.

If this fits your experience, you may feel trapped in a time warp. The child inside you may still be afraid of displeasing parents and other grownups—like in-laws, bosses, supervisors, professors, or significant others. Whether your family set impossible standards or you invented them yourself, your inner rascal may still be striving to be faultless. This internalized demand for perfection can run your life.

In the present

Being our own harshest critic and judge—never loving or accepting ourselves just as we are—is worse than psoriasis or panic attacks. We all know that nagging, judgmental voice inside our heads. It sounds like fingernails on the blackboard. It's usually loudest just after a mishap, before sleep, or early in the morning. Let's call that voice the judge, although harsher names might apply.

The judge says things like the following:

"You should have known better."

"You should have done it better."

"That effort was not up to your potential."

"You missed the boat that time."

"Shame on you."

"You think you're so hot. You blew it."

Without breaking a sweat, your judge can give you 599 ways to be disappointed in yourself. To your judge, you are absolutely never okay. You are guilty as charged, without legal counsel, trial, or jury, just like poor Alice in *Alice in Wonderland*, when the Queen of Hearts screams, "Off with her head!"

The internal battle never ends. The judge roars, "Be perfect. Get it right, stupid!" The kid in us says, "I'm trying. I'll keep trying. I'll do better next time." We need a peacemaker, a mediator, an adult voice inside us who says, "Just hold your horses. I know I'm not perfect. I'm tired of all this conflict. I wish you two would ease up and relax so I can get on with real life."

Once upon a time

Young Jennifer, a very knowledgeable dentist with a busy practice, was asked to give a speech to a group of students. She accepted with confidence, "Yes. Sure. Of course."

Almost immediately, her internal judge began to shout at her. "You don't know enough to make this speech. Now everyone will know you're a fraud. You'd better make it perfect, although I doubt that you can. You need to look better before you get up in front of all those people. Lose those five pounds right now, fatso. Get a haircut. Prepare yourself to answer any questions. Don't make any mistakes. Don't make a fool of yourself. Be perfect."

As her judge voice grew louder, Jennifer became more anxious and uptight. While she ate, while she waited for her next patient, and every time she took a break, she heard her own critical voice like a back seat driver nagging inside her head. She envisioned everything that could go wrong and all the mistakes she could make. Her internal voice kept putting her down while pushing her toward impossible greatness, toward perfection.

Soon she felt frozen and insecure every time she thought about the speech. Her digestion began to suffer. She got hiccups. She itched. The more she told herself to be the perfect speaker, the more impossible everything seemed to be. She got so anxious that she imagined giving up, quitting her practice, packing her bags, leaving her family, and joining the French Foreign Legion, though she knew that wouldn't solve anything. She had to do something different, but she didn't know what.

The very same night that she was deciding which bag to pack for departure to the Sahara, her old dog Socks jumped onto her bed and began to lick her hand. Socks wasn't worried about her speech. He wasn't worried about anything. He didn't know she wasn't perfect, and he didn't care. He was totally fine with himself, his dogginess, and his uncritical love for her. He didn't seem to have any nasty internal voices harping on him. Jennifer scratched Socks behind his ears and realized that he knew something she had forgotten. Even though he looked like an unmade bed, he never doubted his doggy self. He wasn't plagued with anxiety and shame. He knew he was perfectly adequate.

She listened to Socks pant and remembered that she was also adequate in lots of ways. After all, she didn't look like an unmade bed, and she really was a competent dentist, a good mom, a careful driver, an excellent cook, and a responsible dog owner. Even with her judge's voice finding fault inside her head, she could probably manage to speak coherently in front of an audience. They might even like her.

In bed with those thoughts, Jennifer relaxed for the first time in days. Her hiccups stopped. She changed her goal from giving the perfect speech to giving an adequate speech. Her digestion improved. She remembered that she really did know a lot and she could be valuable to students. Her itching stopped. Her confidence began to return. It felt like the tingle in your gums when the shot of Novocaine wears off. She shifted from focusing on herself and her performance to focusing on the task and the audience. After all, the audience was not the enemy. The students would be there to listen and to learn whatever she had to teach them.

During her speech a magical thing happened. After the first five minutes of abject terror, Jennifer relaxed and began to enjoy herself. She lost her self-consciousness, made jokes, and, for the first time since she'd agreed to give the speech, began to have fun. She was far better than she could have imagined, and the students gave her a standing ovation. She had given herself permission to be just who she was, unpressured by any push toward perfection, and adequate to the task at hand. For once, the critical voice in her head had nothing to say.

Most of the time, Jennifer remembers this event. Socks is her live-in reminder. Sometimes she forgets and the judge takes over again. Sometimes hiccups and indigestion tell her that she urgently needs to do something different. Sometimes, when she walks the dog, she can turn down the volume of the relentless voice inside. Sometimes she can turn it off and find some peace. During those moments, the sun shines brighter, and so does she.

Goal

Instead of striving for perfect, work toward adequate, competent, and unique. You really can get there from here. Keep remembering that you are already adequate, you are certainly unique, and you can get to competent—no matter what your inner judge says. Let the concept of good enough into your life. Relax into ordinary.

You probably believe it's okay for other people to be less than perfect. Be as generous to yourself as you are to them. Somehow, they're good enough, and you can love and accept them just the way they are—bumps, lumps, warts, and all. Love and accept yourself just as uncritically.

Stretch yourself

Here are some techniques, tactics, and strategies to help you handle your internal judge.

1. Turn down the volume so you can hear yourself think. Make it softer and softer. Tell the judge, "I hear you. You don't need to shout in my ear."
2. Get that unforgiving voice of the judge outside yourself. Visualize it. Draw it. Sculpt it. Give it a name. Decorate it with feathers, bones, fur, sequins. Make it ugly, gross, a terrible sight to behold. Put it on a dartboard. Sew it on a punching bag. Attach it to a pillow you can kick or throw. Give it a home in the doghouse.
3. Be tough. Talk back to that judge. Whomp it. Make it shrivel. It's a new day in court. Take control.

We regret to inform you that you can't kill the judge. You can't even silence it totally. But you can manage it, tell it who's boss, and make temporary peace with it. Acknowledge that its original task was to protect you. Now you hardly need it any more, especially when it's tyrannical. Helpful or not, the judge is a part of us always. It's our internal companion, a voice left over from earlier days. We need to learn to live with the beast. Tame it. Train it. Be sure it's housebroken.

Affirmations

Here are some of the snacks we promised you. They're like vitamins for an undernourished soul. Take them once a day, more often on bad days. Try them for a week and see if you feel better. If you just feel silly, try them for another week.

I am perfectly imperfect.

Being imperfect is my way of being human.

If I can live with your imperfections, I can live with mine.

My flaws are better than yours.

My imperfections are perfectly normal.

I am worthy, lovable, smart, cute, and entirely imperfect.

I am imperfect without even trying.

I am imperfect; therefore I am.

3

Imperfection Equals Failure?

Myth

Either I do everything perfectly or I'm a worthless failure.

Truth

You don't do everything perfectly and you never did. You're not a worthless failure and you never were. If you've lived long enough, chances are you've failed a test, lost your keys, forgotten your phone number, spilled your drink, and dented a fender. You've probably angered someone, ended a relationship, broken a heart or two, made a mistake, tripped, and fallen. We know this about you. Trust us. We also know this about ourselves.

There are two kinds of people in this world: the kind who think there are two kinds of people, and the kind who know life just ain't that simple. Like life, we are all richer and more complex than either a winner or a loser, right or wrong, good or bad, smart or dumb, thin or fat, loved or unloved, Democrat or Republican, perfect or imperfect. There are always more than two choices, more than two ways of being and seeing things. There are many shades of grey between the

15

black and white. There are always, at the very least, third and fourth options.

Just as one part of life is not all of life, one error, one defect, one tragedy is not everything we are. Some mistakes seem to be disasters, but they are really challenges or opportunities. Some change our lives forever or give us a glimpse of our limitations and our possibilities. Sometimes trouble seems to define us and follow us around like Pigpen's dust cloud, and we feel like "Disasters 'R' Us." Sometimes we forget that we're more than any of the disasters in our lives.

We become like adolescents who think if they have one zit, they can't go out of the house. They're embarrassed. They feel ashamed and despise themselves and hide. The zit takes over. They become their zit and nothing else, the tragic victims in their own teenage dramas. We forget that being human means having zits, being blemished, living with our warts.

Once, when there were no cars and everyone moved through the world on foot or horse or mule, we were all more visible to each other. We saw people with one leg or one eye or one tooth as part of our ordinary landscape. Old folks mixed with young ones, fat folks with thin ones. We saw that people came in all sizes and shapes, with lots of bruises and bumps. Now, except in big cities, most of us move in cars and rarely see a lot of different kinds of people on the street. More and more, our view of other people tends to come from the TV screens in our living rooms.

The media give us neatly packaged images, showing us how life (and we) should be. We learn that people look perfectly beautiful and that life should be easy, effortless, and without mistakes. We learn that any problem can (and should) be resolved before the final commercial. We never see rehearsals, the first-time flop, the trial run, the let's-learn-from-our-mistakes opening night. Only bloopers, played for laughs, remind us that folks on TV are really imperfect, too. But bloopers are used for comic relief, and a reality check to remind us that mistakes are perfectly normal. We forget that quality production takes time, effort, practice, and lots of retakes. Even Beethoven had multiple versions of his fifth symphony before he thought it was good enough. Forget perfect. It's hard enough just to get things right.

The demanding, gritty work that people do is rarely visible anymore. Things seem to just happen. It's easy to forget that before that fish bedded down in its Styrofoam tray and snuggled under the clear plastic wrap many, many people toiled long and hard to bring it to our neighborhood grocery. Somewhere, people put on their windbreakers, boarded a boat, chugged out into an ocean, dropped their nets, and pulled out a lot of unusual things, including the fish you're planning to have for dinner. Someone cleaned, gutted, and filleted it. Someone's clothes smelled awful. Someone packed it in ice and trucked it to the market. Someone garnished it with parsley. We see none of the process, only the slick, smooth, finished product. Some of us even forget that fish come from water. They look so picture perfect in their little trays in the supermarket that we can imagine they were born without heads, tails, or bones. We can imagine that apples come already waxed, without bruises or hailstone marks or wormholes. And just imagine what we can imagine about milk and steak.

The tidy, sterile, prepackaged world seems so flawless on TV and in supermarkets that we seem to be the only ones in the world who still have defects. Our fear of flawing makes us curse our imperfections, hide them, and deny them. We pad them, lift them, reject them, or erase them. We forget that there's no such thing as a flaw-free world or a flawless human. We should have a tag tied to us when we are born, that carries this reminder: "Any flaws you find in this human's fabric are an integral part of the weave. Variations in shading are intentional and only enhance the quality of the design."

Once upon a time

The 1974 film *The Stepford Wives* was set in the neat and tidy suburb of Stepford, Connecticut. In Stepford, all the husbands were perfectly tended by their perfect wives. The homes were perfect. The meals were perfect. The sex was perfect. The happy husbands wallowed in all this perfection, having killed off their human, imperfect wives one by one and replaced them with robots. The robots looked just like the wives, but they were electronic, flawless, and maintenance-free—the ideal fantasy wives, perfectly programmed and exquisitely responsive. They just weren't human. In fact, they were too good to be real.

Too much upgrading toward perfection can turn any of us into a Stepford wife (or husband). We can struggle to destroy and replace untidy aliveness with high-tech precision and electronics. We can even deprogram our most basic human wiring. We can endlessly retrofit ourselves, envying those stainless steel models who never make mistakes, and never trip over their own extension cords. We can strive to be entirely perfect and very dead.

In the beginning

New babies have no concept of mistakes and no problems with self-esteem. They're just fine with themselves. They're born unaware of what's okay and what's not. By nature, kids are blank tapes with no internal critical or judgmental voices. They plunge into life knowing no rules, no manners, no orderliness. They don't know the proper ways to look, feel, act, or be. They have a lot to discover. In the beginning they learn many things in simple terms: yes or no, good or bad, hot or cold, okay or not okay. It takes years and some maturity to realize how much lies between the two extremes. Learning about the full range of responses takes time, practice, and lots of lumps, bruises, and hard knocks. We get it and we forget it, and we have to get it again and again.

Some grownups view kids as faulty little adults who make a lot of mistakes and need endless correction. But when kids are continually judged and corrected, they begin to doubt themselves and see themselves as flawed. They learn to hate and judge their own imperfections and mistakes, to despise their slings and errors, and to loathe themselves. They try to do better, and to be better. They become anxious about not getting it right the first time and worry about failing.

The trouble is, we all learned by making mistakes. We took risks and failed, took risks and failed, took risks and succeeded. We fell down a lot before we learned to walk. We needed, and still need, encouragement to experiment, to learn from failure and success. It's never easy being a kid figuring out how to be a grownup. (It's not even easy being a grownup figuring out how to be a grownup.)

Even the best parents are imperfect. They make mistakes, too. Often they don't separate a child's actions from the child. Their message is one of judgment rather than an offer of information about the child's behavior. Rather than say, "Don't eat the plant," they say, "Bad boy!" Instead of "Good sharing," they say, "Good girl!" Instead of "This is how you clean up spilled milk," they say, "Clumsy! Why did you do that? What's the matter with you, anyway?"

Parents may not see any difference between those messages. But to a child those messages may mean that they, not their actions, are good or bad, right or wrong. Children judge themselves as they feel judged. All too easily, they turn "You made a mistake" into "I *am* a mistake," and carry that misunderstanding for the rest of their lives.

Sometimes mothers make simple, reasonable requests like, "Pick up your clothes," and "Don't track mud on the rug." And sometimes kids (in true kid fashion) feel their primal self-worth attacked. They translate those requests into, "I'm a terrible slob," and "I can't do anything right." Twenty years later, a female roommate says, "Company is coming. Could you pick up your stuff and move it out of the living room?" The young man hears, "You're a lazy, inconsiderate slob," and translates that into, "I can never do anything right." He responds, "Don't tell me what to do! You're not my mother!"

This kind of kid translation can sneak unexpectedly into our grownup brains. When we hear a simple request for action as a negative judgment on ourselves, we can overreact and respond like an angry child. It's no wonder that many an innocent roommate has been bowled over by bewildering tantrums.

Some well-intentioned families think they're doing the right thing by encouraging competitiveness and comparing their children to siblings and other kids. "What's wrong with you? Why aren't you as clean, clever, careful, as Clara?" Children hear this and perceive themselves at the low end of the seesaw. "If Joey is the good kid, I must be the bad kid." "If Mary is the smart one, I must be the dumb one." "If Patti is the pretty one, I must be the homely one." "If George is Daddy's favorite, then what am I?" Comparisons encourage kids to think like seesaws—either you're up or you're down. If someone else is put at the top, kids can feel stuck at the bottom.

Almost all parents aspire to be perfect parents. Some only feel adequate when their children seem perfect (just the way their parents wanted them to be). They can't allow their little ones (or big ones) to make mistakes. These are the parents who give kids a hard time when they get only ninety-nine on the math test, when they don't hit a home run each time they're at bat, or when they don't get into medical school. These parents think they're being helpful by encouraging their kids to be the best, but in actuality they're often instilling self-doubt, shame, and a belief that any imperfection means failure. Perfectionism can be inherited along with the family silver, the blue-chip stocks, and the weak ankles.

Even if our parents didn't have a thousand yardsticks to measure us, everyone else did. Our pediatricians did: Were we the perfect weight for our age and height or were we puny? Our teachers did: Were we reading at the right level or were we asked to repeat third grade? Was our IQ score high enough or were we below average? Our priests or ministers did: Were we going to heaven or bound for hell? Often no one told us there was anything between absolutely right and terribly wrong, so it felt impossible to measure up. It's no wonder so many kids feel less than okay, inadequate, and full of self-doubt. It's amazing so many of us turned out so well.

In the present

As adults, we often see what's wrong in ten-foot-tall, red-hot neon letters. What's right looks like the small print at the bottom of the page. One rejection and we feel totally unlovable. One fight and we think our marriage is ruined. Five pounds gained and we feel fat and ugly. Our kid's not a doctor, so we've failed as parents. When we get eighty-seven compliments and one complaint, we often remember and obsess about the complaint. We can allow one negative ion to change our whole atomic structure.

Once upon a time

A sophisticated twenty-eight-year-old woman named Karen was tall, graceful, and attractive, with many friends and accomplishments. Life seemed to flow easily for her. She never waited long for the next job or the next boyfriend. Ordinary troubles seemed to slide off her elegant Teflon exterior. She seemed content.

One night when the moon was full, she was out drinking white wine with her best friend, Patricia, who was six inches shorter and ten pounds heavier than Karen. We'll never know whether it was the wine, the moon, or a rare sense of safety, but Karen began to weep. Into

Patricia's sympathetic ear, she poured some of her inner turmoil. Beneath her elegant facade, Karen had always felt ugly and unattractive. She was ashamed of having such small breasts. She felt that if her breasts were not enough, surely she was not enough. Karen admitted she'd always dressed to hide her insecurity. She hated the swimming pool. She felt awkward about sex. She'd covered, camouflaged, and padded. She pumped iron. But still she felt inferior, almost deformed.

When she was an adolescent, her father teased her about being flat as a board, like a boy. Her older sister made fun of her when she wanted a bra. A former boyfriend made pointed jokes about breasts. She imagined that every reference to breast size was really about her. She was trying to decide whether to get breast implants, even though they might be dangerous. Karen wondered whether Patricia thought implants would enhance her self-esteem enough to be worth the risk.

Patricia was shocked speechless. She'd always thought Karen looked fabulous. She'd never imagined her elegant friend would have concerns about her body. "I think you're fine just the way you are," she said, at last.

"I don't want to hear it," Karen retorted. "You just don't understand."

"You're probably right. I don't understand. I'd trade bodies with you in a second!"

Silence ensued. Patricia was on the wrong track. Karen blew her nose.

"Is there any part of your body you do like?" Patricia asked, in a flash of genuine perceptiveness.

Karen thought a minute. She admitted that she really liked her hair and her eyes. Her teeth were okay. Her legs were good, and her nails were strong. The list kept growing.

"So there's a lot you do like," Patricia said.

Karen looked up. "I guess so. I'd forgotten how much of myself I really wouldn't change. In fact, almost all of me is just fine. I've been really healthy all my life. Maybe silicone is just too high a price to pay."

"So you've been hating your whole body just because of that old business about your breasts? Would you like to trade bodies?" Patricia asked.

Karen smiled. "I don't think so, but thanks for not laughing. And I will buy you another glass of wine."

There were light years between how others saw and judged Karen and how she saw and judged herself. She was so focused on what was missing that she lost sight of what was there. Her cup really was more than half full.

When we believe that we are flawed, we shrink from compliments, praise, or acceptance. We can't even hear positive words when the old "I'm not good enough" tape is playing in our heads. Friends seem deluded and uninformed when they see us differently than the way we see ourselves. We treat compliments like lint and brush them off. Like Karen, our smooth exteriors may look untroubled while the child inside us feels blemished, unlovable, and untrusting.

Goal

Accept that you are flawed and have accumulated hundreds of frequent failure miles. Make friends with your flaws. Your blemishes may be the most interesting, unique parts of you.

Reevaluate. You can't have everything. *Vogue* models are renowned for their flat chests. Looking like a clothes hanger shows designer fashions to their best advantage.

Appreciate your imperfect self. Accept the kindness of others. You deserve a break after all these years.

Judge all of yourself generously when parts of you fall short. You can fail a statistics exam, a driving test, or a supervisor's evaluation without being stupid. You can lose beauty contests, lovers, and jobs without being ugly.

Accept the inevitable. Things will go wrong. Your car will. Your cat will. Your hair will. Your body will. You will.

Stretch yourself

Whenever you feel like a total failure, make a list of fourteen things you accomplished that day. Keep it simple. You probably brushed your teeth, walked without falling down, boiled an egg, wrote a complete sentence, thought a complete thought, worked the microwave, dialed the phone, poured a cup of coffee without spilling it, fed the cat, and countless others. Basics do count. They remind you of how much you know and how accomplished you really are. Remind yourself often. Let others remind you, too.

Beware of destructive either/or thinking. You're not a total failure and you're not entirely perfect. Use rose-colored bifocals. Focus on the positive. Soften and blur the negative.

Let yourself be congratulated. Congratulate yourself. Pat yourself on the back. Brag a little. Squeal with delight. Take compliments much more seriously than you take criticism.

Spend a few minutes at the end of each day—preferably while soaking in a warm bubble bath—and run through every sweet, pleasant, good thing that happened in the last twenty-four hours. Be specific. Let yourself relive it. This may be a little painful at first, like coming out of a dark room into the sun. Allow time for your eyes to adjust. Enjoy.

Delight in your mistakes. Laugh at your failures. Turn them into human-interest stories. Share them. Exaggerate them. People love to hear that others goof up too.

Allow yourself moments, even days, of premeditated and deliberate imperfection. For instance, you could expand your repertoire by experimenting with these less-than-perfect activities:

Wear two different-colored socks.

Let nothing match. (Plaids and flowers are good.)

Respond to a question with, "I don't know."

Take a wrong turn.

Get lost.

Ask for help at least once a day.

Start a local chapter of Imperfects Anonymous.

Be silly.

Be frivolous.

Tell a bad joke badly.

Laugh at yourself.

Laugh with yourself.

Let others laugh, too.

Add many other silly activities to your own list. Share it with an imperfect friend. Go out and play in the imperfect world. You will not be tested on this material.

Affirmations

I fondly accept my imperfections.
I have fabulous flaws.
My flaws make me unique and therefore priceless.
Love me; love my flaws.
I am greater than any one part of me.
I'm always a partial success.
I'm totally lovable, even though he or she or they don't love me.
I'm flawed; therefore I am.

4

Something Is Wrong with Me?

Myth

I should feel strong and confident all the time.
If I don't, there must be something wrong with me.

Truth

No one feels confident and strong all the time. If they do, there's something wrong with them.

Feelings come and go. It is what we think about them that makes them either acceptable or not, and makes us either okay or not okay with ourselves. Some of us learned to judge our anger, grief, or fear, to disallow those feelings someone told us were bad. Some of us had to shrink into calm, cool, and collected and keep all passions under control. Some of us learned to fear frailty, pain, or excitement. We learned never to look foolish, crazy, weak, or vulnerable, and never to admit suffering from PMS.

A young John Wayne was our model. He was the cowboy who never got mad at his horse or showed fear when the bad guys surrounded the cabin. He never cried when he left his woman. He hardly looked back. He was tough, a no-nonsense man of few words. He was nobody's fool. And nobody's mate. "I love ya, darlin', but I got cattle to run up Wyoming way. See you next fall, maybe, if they don't catch up with me in Dodge."

The lone macho cowboy stays manly inside a narrow, safe range of feelings. He never looks out of control. Unlike the rest of us, he never raises tempers, causes confrontation, upsets the dog, or weeps in the dining room. But he's not a real person. Real people experience feelings that tell us what we really care about and what we couldn't care less about. They are an essential and useful part of the human condition, no matter what we learned in the movies.

Some feelings are more comfortable than others, but they all send us messages we couldn't live without—about danger, pleasure, loss, comfort, excess. They remind us to pull our hands away from the hot stove, move toward pleasure and away from pain, eat when we're hungry and stop when we're full. Anger can tell us that some boundary has been violated, sadness that we've lost something precious, weakness that we need to rest. All feelings are teachers.

Every culture has rules about which feelings and actions are appropriate and acceptable for each gender, age, and event. In some places, mourners are encouraged to wail, beat their breasts, and throw themselves on coffins. In other places, grief is hidden behind a veil and only delicate sniffles are tolerated. Some cultures encourage wild dancing, all-night drumming, loud singing, and shouting. Some cultures use broad gestures when they talk, raise their voices in pleasure and in pain, belly laugh, and genuinely reveal themselves.

However, most of us were taught not to express ourselves quite so vividly. The decorum, diplomacy, and discretion preferred in American life mean the British were our cultural models, not the Italians. Good manners meant we had to sniff (not sob), complain (not rant and rave), and titter (not belly laugh). The lace handkerchief was not designed for energetic displays of grief. We learned to value stiff upper lips, stoicism, and containment.

When strong emotions scare us, we don't want to be bothered by them; we never learn what our feelings have to teach us, or how to live with them. We try to send them away, but they keep coming back, like unwanted advertisements stuck inside the screen door. Some feelings stack up on the front porch until we're afraid they'll bury us if we open the door. Others sneak in through the mailbox slot of our dreams. They refuse to leave until we listen to what they have to say about ourselves, our history, and our current circumstances. Unacknowledged feelings can be so pesky, so necessary.

Let's face it. Unhappiness, sadness, confusion, and fear are frequent guests in all of our lives. Expect them. Their visits are natural, normal, and inevitable. They do leave of their own accord—sometimes soon, sometimes not so soon. And we can't always control how long they stay. Usually the less we resist their company, the shorter the visit. Sometimes, when we allow emotions in, they stay longer than we had planned. We never know how long it will take to stop hurting.

It can take six months to more than a year for the physical body to heal from most traumas. To heal a wounded heart or soul can take even longer. The two-aspirin quick fix will work for most headaches, but heartaches like death or divorce require stronger medicine and lots more time. That time heals all wounds is mostly true, but sometimes we need more time than we could have imagined. In the long run, it's easier to invite feelings in than to lock them out. In the short run, too.

There are times when it's wise to contain ourselves and defer feelings. This is especially helpful when winning really matters. In times of war, poker, contact sports, or business, serious players stay calm, cool, collected, calculating, and in control. In those situations, intelligence, survival skills, and mastery are all that count. The smart poker player wants the other players too intimidated to call her bluff, especially if she only has a pair of fours.

Traditional rules of power advise: Don't let them know what you're thinking, feeling, or planning. Keep 'em in the dark. Appear independent, self-sufficient, invincible. Reveal nothing. Remain silent and mysterious or fluff your feathers to show off your size and strength. Take care of business.

But strategies that work brilliantly in competitions and help us succeed as power brokers can cause big trouble at home. John Wayne's strong, silent tactics have limited appeal in bed or other safe and intimate places. Those tactics are best left for the standoff, the poker table, the football field, the conference table, or the war zone.

No matter what the circumstances, life—that rogue challenger of flexibility—will send us powerful events and feelings that demand to be felt. When that happens, we need to figure out how to sit tall and ride across those badlands, even while we're feeling tense, anxious, and frightened under our ten-gallon hats.

We can fake courage and good cheer, keep our chaps on and our spurs jingling, but our bodies know the truth and demand their ransom. Too much constriction and containment can foster saddle sores and various dark green diseases. High blood pressure, low back pain, headaches, indigestion, and colitis all have some emotional components. Life's not so easy for the easy rider after all. Our bodies will react and respond to the heat of our passions even when we think we're being totally cool.

In the beginning

Each family has its own rules about feelings. As children, unfortunately, we all heard some variation on these themes:

"Don't be a baby."

"Stop crying, or I'll give you something to cry about."

"Pull yourself together."

"Don't get so excited. Settle down."

"Don't be so sensitive."

"Don't you raise your voice to me!"

"Don't snivel!"

"Don't look at me like that!"

"When you calm down, we'll talk."

"It didn't hurt that much."

"Grow up."

"Don't be a sissy!"

These kinds of family messages shame children for having and expressing strong feelings. When families reject feelings, children learn to reject them, too. They join their parents and distance themselves from their own emotions. They can learn to hate, ignore, hide, and disown their feelings. They learn to monitor themselves carefully and to stay within the range of family acceptability.

Kids learn early to pretend to be cool. Boys, especially, learn that it's never okay to cry. Girls learn that it's never okay to get angry. When feelings go underground, kids can get depressed, withdraw, or act out in all sorts of imaginative and unexpected ways at home, at school, and in the neighborhood.

In many families, feelings are divided up and parceled out so each family member gets to claim and manifest only one. One person will have the corner on depression, another on rage, another on humor, another on sensitivity. We often get stuck with the feelings no one else has claimed. Think about who carried which feelings in your family, which ones were not okay for you to feel, which ones were yours alone.

Once upon a time

Matthew's father was charming at work and to the world at large. But when he came home, he turned into the lone rager. He'd walk into the house a ticking time bomb, and no one ever knew what would set him off. Without warning, he'd go berserk, yelling, screaming, threatening, and throwing things. He intimidated everyone. No one dared to cross him. No one dared to ask for anything. Matthew's father had the corner on anger and rage while his mother, terrified, hid in the corner and wept.

His tantrums seemed like a herd of wild buffalo stampeding through the house. Even after the dust settled, everyone tiptoed cautiously around him. For Matthew, there was no model for anger that wasn't life threatening. He never learned that he could feel deeply without being intimidating, could express anger without being dangerous. He had no place to express his feelings, no help in developing internal controls. Matthew was left to choose between never showing his anger like Mom, or becoming a fearsome rage-aholic like Dad.

In the present

Most of us learned that feelings are unacceptable, so it's no surprise that strong displays of emotion are often labeled frightening, out of control, hysterical, or potentially dangerous. Sometimes they are, but mostly, they're not. Angry sparks between consenting adults usually last only three minutes, although the smoke may last for days and the slow burn even longer.

Adults who were frightened by explosive rages when they were children can feel stuck in the old terror of the vulnerable child. They will do anything to avoid emotional explosions, both in themselves and in others. Responsible adults have to develop good internal controls to allow and accept strong feelings. Grownups who are neither aggressors nor victims set healthy limits, are emotionally responsible, and know when to use the smoke alarm.

We so-called civilized adults have lots of fancy ways to protect ourselves from feelings. Sometimes we intellectualize them away by talking ourselves out of what we feel: Feeling this won't solve anything, so why bother? Don't think about it. Just let it go. Forget it. Time will take care of it. Talking never accomplishes anything. No sense crying over spilled milk.

Sometimes we use drugs to avoid feelings. Jerome, a recovering alcoholic, admitted that it took two years of sobriety to learn to experience and cope with all the sensations that alcohol and other drugs had masked. He was shocked at how much he hadn't experienced during his alcoholic years. He said, "I'm feeling all the time now, and I don't even have names for a lot of the stuff that's happening to me." At first, his own wife didn't recognize his responses. He didn't, either. He hadn't felt winter in such a long time that he was surprised to find himself cold in February. He was learning to live SOBER, learning to feel again. S.O.B.E.R. stands for "Son of a bitch! Everything's real!"

Sometimes we use compulsive behaviors to distract us from feelings. We numb our anxiety, pain, or sense of emptiness with excessive shopping, eating, exercise, working, gambling, or doing. Sometimes we even fill our lives with crises and chaos so we won't experience anything but franticness. When we're very busy, just keeping up, barely coping, then there's no time to feel, or deal with real feelings.

Sometimes we create socially acceptable masks for unacceptable feelings. We become sarcastic instead of angry, bitter and blaming instead of sad and disappointed. We become bored or depressed instead of angry and helpless. We hide behind humor and cleverness instead of appearing vulnerable.

Sometimes when we don't let ourselves feel much of anything, denied and delayed emotions insist on coming out anyway. We're angry at the boss, so we kick the dog. We haven't cried over the loss of a love, so we kick the dog. Our marriage is failing, so we kick the dog. When we displace our feelings, rather than deal with our own misery, we kick the trusty dog (or any loyal and available creature). Eventually most abused creatures will bite or run away.

When we can allow the full spectrum of emotions in ourselves and in others, we can let ourselves be intimate. Intimacy is about feeling safe enough to share our tears, joy, rage, spontaneity, passion, pride, and tenderness. Intimacy means becoming more visible, more vulnerable, less protected, and more open to learning about our true natures. It means trusting and being trustworthy.

It takes courage to reveal ourselves. Old people, people who have brushed death, or very alive and creative people are often our best models for living spontaneous and unconventional lives. They are not afraid to hang their socially acceptable masks on a hook at the back of the closet while they do their own thing, no matter what society says. They allow themselves to be, to feel and to show their feelings, to be mellow, to be outrageous, to laugh, to be unreasonable. They know there's little time to waste, so they celebrate their own vitality.

Goal

Feel whatever you feel and choose how to act. Maintain your equilibrium. Encourage others to maintain theirs. Honor your childhood distress. Respect your adult choices.

Be imperfect and feel your feelings. Choose your own face, your own mask, your own rhythm, mood, and temperament. You look good on you.

When the wild horsemen of the emotional world—like rage, grief, or terror—chase you across your neat and tidy life, keep them from stampeding you, running you over, or dragging you in the mud. Welcome them. Give them some oats. Let them graze a while and fertilize your yard. Get to know them. Be nice to them and let them go on their way. They'll be back, but they never stay for long if you stroke them. If you don't, they can hang around forever and eat you out of house and home.

Stretch yourself

No feeling has to last forever, nor will it. Just feel it, and the feeling changes (eventually). Just talk about it, and the feeling changes (eventually). In an hour, a day, or even a week, we move through the full range of feelings from terrific to terrible. We spend much time in the middle. Happiness is not a permanent state. Neither is unhappiness. Neither is neutral.

Find a playmate and playact those feelings you never got to practice. Let yourself be unhappy, angry, unreasonable, difficult, weak, tired, ecstatic, satisfied. Try on all kinds of masks.

When you feel upset, call a friend and complain. Let yourself be nurtured. Nurture yourself. Wallow a little in your unhappiness. Ask for kindness. Be as understanding and kind to yourself as you would be to any friend in distress.

Decide how many hours of misery you really need in a given week. Then indulge yourself. If the dog dies, give yourself permission to cry for as long as you need. When you're ready, finish, get out, work out, and get on with life. Repeat as often as necessary.

Affirmations

I'm imperfect and I have feelings.
I can feel whatever I feel.
I will let my feelings teach me.
I don't have to be confident or strong all the time.
I can choose to be miserable.
I choose when and where to show my feelings.
I can choose how to act and react.
Give me feelings or give me death.
I feel; therefore I am.

5

True Love and Living Happily Ever After?

Myth

I will ride off into the sunset with my one true love and
we will live happily ever after in the palace on the hill.

Truth

There may be some things you've overlooked. Palaces on the hill have
large mortgages. The horse will need oats. It will get dark. It will rain.

In truth, you will kiss a lot of frogs before you find a prince(ss).
Once, when we stayed in the same town for a lifetime, we connected
with frogs and royal persons who swam in the same pond, and everybody knew their swimming styles and their warts. Now, because we all
move around from puddle to pool to pond, we don't have any history
with the local frogs. They're more likely to be strangers our mothers
never knew. Now, it's hard to tell who's a frog, who's a prince(ss), and
who's pretending to be a toad. Now, more than ever, background
checks are required.

Although we never forget our first frog, we usually don't hop off with it. Before we're too old, we find that we've loved a lot of amphibians—some for a long time, some for a short time. Usually, they turned out to be more than frogs and less than royalty.

For those of us in love with romance, the hunt for perfect frogs goes on forever. We dream of that magic moment when we first see our beloved across a crowded room. A chorus of violins begins to sing, and all movements have the gentle grace of slow motion. In a golden glow, softly focused, our one true love waltzes into our open arms and plants the perfect kiss on our waiting lips. The snap, crackle, and pop of endorphins can be heard around the world. The earth trembles. We dance until dawn, tenderly staring into each other's eyes. Then we are wafted off to Tahiti to live on the beach, untroubled, happily ever after, in perfect bliss and harmony. This romantic dream is so effortless, so smooth, and so intoxicating, it's better than drugs or chocolate. It's what we've been waiting for: one enchanted evening to transport us out of our ordinary days into a lifetime of ecstasy.

We love this story and we hate to give it up. It lives on in fairy tales, Hollywood, musical comedy, popular songs, trashy novels, steamy novels, great novels. It's a story about courtship, about seduction, about honeymoons. It celebrates chemistry and hormones and the moment of euphoria that lasts forever. The message is that love is so magical that it doesn't need to be based on friendship, time spent together, shared interests, good talk, or similar values. It will just come, willed by fate, past life experiences, kismet, karma, or destiny.

The story tells us these two frogs were meant to be together. Maybe they were; maybe they will live happily ever after. But maybe they'll learn some of the things the stories don't talk about: how life changes over time; how to cope with the ups and downs of life's little jokes; how to cultivate patience, good humor, and tenderness; how to keep a little bit of magic around the house.

The old stories can keep us in love with love. They encourage us to dress our frog as a prince(ss) and blind ourselves to warts and bulging eyes. We can fall in love with our own creations and deny slimy reality until it slaps us in the face. Caution: When our royal beloveds seem absolutely perfect (Look, Mom, I made a prince[ss]!) we probably invented them. Sometimes our royal beloveds have invented themselves.

Once upon a time

Janet was twenty-five, a serious and dedicated student just finishing her Ph.D. in physics, when she met Sam, a well-known and charismatic visiting professor from another university. He was fifty-five, married, with two teenage children and a small baby. Sam and Janet worked together on a project, and daily and appreciatively he told her how bright and capable she was. Janet worked even harder, determined to be an excellent student and earn his praise. He began to comment on what she was wearing, how her hair shone, and how radiant her skin was. Janet started coming to school earlier and earlier, checking herself in the mirror before Sam arrived. She was sparked by his caring and turned on by his charm. His project became her focus. His work became her passion. Before very long, she was short circuited and thrown completely off balance.

SHAZAAM! There was enough electricity in the physics lab to propel them directly into bed. He was sophisticated and experienced. He spent as much time admiring her body as he did making love. They began working together in the evenings. She was totally smitten. Her glow was incandescent. She felt she had found her true love. Within a month, Janet was imagining church weddings and picket fences.

Sam hinted that he might be willing to leave his wife and children to be with her. She longed to take him seriously, but the facts kept gnawing at her. After all, she had been trained in the scientific method. Sam's current wife was his third. She, too, had been a student of his. They had met while he was a visiting professor. When he talked about his wives, he whined that they had never understood him. He was demeaning and critical of his marriages.

In her saner moments, Janet envisioned history repeating itself. One day in the not-so-distant future, he would be nasty, demeaning, and critical as he described her to his next female graduate assistant. She began to suspect some slime under his princely demeanor. She was only the princess of the moment. She would become just one more distraught female in the long line of broken-hearted young women who had loved him. But she was torn. Was this love? (Not.) Would it be different this time, as he assured her it would be? (Not.) Could she let him go? (Not easily. Ouch.) Could she keep him? (No way.) Was he really an untrustworthy cad? (He was.)

Janet was deeply in love for the first time, and Sam was deeply in lust one more time. Fortunately, Janet's brain zapped her in time and was able to override her heart's longing. In a blinding moment of piercing clarity and good judgment, she said good-bye. And she cried a lot. No more Sam-and-Janet evenings.

Sam's princely gift to her was that he had respected her brains and uncovered her sensuality. She knew now that her neurons fired in more complex and interesting ways than she had imagined. A sleeping part of her had been awakened. She was ready now for a partner who told the whole truth about his princeliness and his frogginess. She was ready for someone with whom she could be both smart and sexy, who would honor all of her for the long term, not just one short semester. A dangerous princely cad, like Sam, sees the beautiful princess, admires her, seizes her, releases her, and inevitably hops off to the next lily pad. He doesn't want to spend time understanding or regretting the trail of tears he leaves behind him.

Sondheim's prince says it best in the musical *Into the Woods*: "But darling, I was trained to be charming, not sincere." Abruptly, he exits stage left.

In the beginning

Our first experience and understanding of love came from our earliest bonding. We had no sense of who we were then, no ego boundaries, no awareness of where we ended and our beloved caretakers began. We were fused. Growing up meant separating, individuating, recognizing that we could be independent and self-sufficient. But in doing so, we lost that completely safe, oceanic first attachment. Often, a part of us still longs for that lost, basic, primal connection. When we are euphoric, first falling in love, we come close. We remember how it felt. Nothing could possibly be better.

Children know when they feel loved. They get messages from hands, eyes, voices, arms, breath. They know who handles them gently, who speaks to them softly, who plays joyfully with them, and who protects them. Unconditional love gives them permission to be exactly who they are. It creates safety. A reliable, caring world encourages children to flower into secure, benevolent, self-confident adults.

Children know when they don't feel loved, when something is missing. Most of us didn't have perfectly idyllic, secure beginnings. Some holes in the loving blankets that we were wrapped in somehow never got mended. Chilly and insecure, we often sought warmth and safety within ourselves. We began to doubt we would ever be cared for and often decided we were undeserving and unlovable. Now, when we take lovers, we ask them to make up for whatever we missed as children. We want them to have the perfect thread and needles to mend the holes from our childhood and keep us forever warm and protected. Alas, no one person, no team of people, however loving, can make up for most childhood disappointments. That is our own inner work—to come to peace about the world we came from, to thrive in the world we now live in, to love and to let love in.

In the present

As adults we try to make up for the disappointments of childhood. We try to get our needs met by making relationships that look very much like the ones we knew as children. We often choose partners and marriages like the ones we knew best. Even when we swear we'll never have a relationship like that of our parents and we choose very different kinds of mates, we find ourselves living the same familiar patterns. No matter how unsatisfying, it feels like home, like Mom, like Dad, like some version of our first family—familiar. There's no place like home.

Sometimes while we're waiting for the perfect mate, we're working to look younger, sexier, more alluring, seductive, and attractive. We cast spells to entice our one true love. We buy potions and lotions, weights and tonics, fatteners and thinners, but what we're really buying is hope. We hope that this product or that service will make true love happen. Advertisements keep reminding us that for a small (or very large) price, we can all be magically alluring. If we just buy their priceless products, companies tell us, we will become thin, fit, handsome enough, with no dandruff, headaches, or static cling. After we've purchased and consumed hope in its many forms, Mr. or Ms. Right will come along and see that we are the perfect soulmate and stay forever. This witchery is cooked up on Madison Avenue and we're all susceptible to it. Hucksters know what sells, and hope is the irresistible product.

37

Sometimes we long for connection so deeply that we imagine every relationship as a possible true love. Hating to be alone, we see the world so full of happy couples that we attach ourselves to almost anyone. We overlook all faults, all handwriting on the wall, all of our friends' groans, all of our parents' fears. We forget that even the most toxic and abusive relationships begin with honeymoons. We can be blinded by love and land flat on our faces when we realize that our fairy-tale romance was written by Stephen King.

Waiting for her beloved blinds many a woman to the realities of love. Eyes closed, like Sleeping Beauty she slumbers, waiting for someone to discover her and wake her from her long sleep. Surely a handsome prince will arrive, love her unconditionally, and transform her into a vibrant, secure, creative, happy, fulfilled woman. She's on hold, waiting for the phone to ring. She can't take work or college seriously because she's listening for the hoof beats of a white horse.

This profound fairy tale is a Western archetype. It keeps women snoozing, waiting for deliverance. It can be very hard to take on the challenges of a career, a new living situation, or an independent life when the culture says "Wait for the right guy; sleep until he comes along. Don't be a doctor, marry one."

Once upon a time

Today, new fairy tales are challenging the traditional models. *The Paper Bag Princess*, by Robert N. Munsch, tells of the beautiful Princess Elizabeth who was going to marry Prince Ronald. Then a terrible fiery dragon smashed her castle, burned her expensive clothes, and carried off Prince Ron. In this emergency, Elizabeth could find only a paper bag to wear. Nevertheless, she chased after the dangerous beast. When she found the dragon's cave, he told her to go away. He was too tired and sleepy to eat her after his busy day burning up castles and forests. But Elizabeth persisted and tricked the weary dragon into showing off his great power. She challenged him to burn up one hundred forests. He did. She tricked him into showing how he could fly around the world in ten seconds. He did. She outsmarted the dragon by wearing him out. Exhausted, he fell dead asleep.

Quietly, Elizabeth entered the cave to rescue Prince Ronald.

Instead of being relieved and grateful to be rescued, he complained that she looked a mess! She smelled like ashes. Her hair was all tangled, and she was wearing a dirty old paper bag. He told her to come back when she was dressed like a real princess. Elizabeth told Ronald that his clothes were pretty, his hair was neat, and he did look like a real prince, but he was really a bum. She didn't want to marry him after all. The end.

Imagine what life would be like if the brave, wide-awake Elizabeth had been our model of the perfect woman instead of Sleeping Beauty!

Some people spend much of their lives waiting for the perfect prince(ss). Nothing less than perfection will do. They reject any froggy mortal who tries to enter their castle. A badly calibrated frog detector can misread people who look a little green and send them on their way before anyone recognizes their golden character, crowning intellect, or royal sense of humor. "I won't even have coffee with her!" "He's just not marriage material." You never know. An unknown green stranger might not be the love of your life, but he or she might be a great friend, a terrific Scrabble partner, or someone to dance with on Tuesday nights. It might be useful to give folks more than one chance. If they don't turn out okay, you can always drop them into the nearest pond.

Sometimes we discard people before they discard us. We've been so wounded that our egos shudder at the thought of another rejection. It hurt then, and it hurts every time. It takes a brave soul to venture into unknown waters. So we all need life preservers, reliable arms of friends to keep us afloat when we feel like we're drowning. The only way never to sink, never to get hurt, is to take no risks, stay on familiar turf, never get wet, and avoid frog ponds entirely—a safe, dry, and lonely choice.

Goal

Accept that you will not always be in love. Sometimes, you'll have no romance in sight. You will be alone. These are times to stay awake, to thrive, and to love and nurture your own soul, your unique and distinct life, just as it is. This doesn't have to mean you're deprived of love. Love is not a scarce commodity. Expand your definition to include the love of friends, relatives, playmates, the gods, mother nature, pets, art, laughter, rainbows, and hot fudge. You never need to feel deprived of love. It's everywhere. Keep your frog detector calibrated so it clicks when someone or something real, loving, and lovable comes along.

Stretch yourself

If, at this moment in your life, you are in love, saddling up to ride off into the sunset, hold your horses. Make sure your heart and head are on the same team. Stop and examine your new love's old baggage—history, friendships, parents, children, spending habits, addictions. Be realistic. History tends to repeat itself. You will be the newest chapter in a very long story. Be sure it's a story you want to be in.

If you think you're being blinded by romance, take this jiffy pop quiz.

Delusional Bliss Pop Quiz
Instructions: Check all responses that apply.
1. Have you given up
   ___ your other loves?
   ___ going to the gym?
   ___ eating?
   ___ talking to the goldfish?
   ___ spending time with friends?
   ___ changing the furnace filter?
2. Have you given up yourself?___
3. Are you spending lots of time
   ___ waiting for the call, the roses, the valentine, the next date?
   ___ wondering what your beloved really thinks, feels, wants?
   ___ wishing for some sign that he or she really cares?
   ___ inventing a prince(ss) when he or she is mostly a slimy toad?

If you checked any of these responses, you're probably in deep delusional bliss. Take a deep breath and ask your best friends for a reality check. You might just have fallen for a toad because you are so in love with being in love. It's easy to do, when you're a wild and crazy romantic.

True Love and Living Happily Ever After?

If you do decide to ride off into the sunset with the froggy prince(ss), keep in touch with the other loves in your life. If your head is in the clouds, be sure your feet are on the ground.

Affirmations

I can love someone deeply and hold onto myself.
I can love someone and keep my sense of humor.
Frogs may come and frogs may go, but I will never leave me.
I am a prince(ss) with or without a partner.
My delusions are just not what they used to be.
My vision of romance may be a little out of date.
When I am alone I'm still cute, loveable, smart, attractive, and free.
I'm a frog and a prince(ss); therefore I am.

6

Father Knows Best?

Myth

Father knows best and/or mother knows best.

Truth

This outdated TV show, an echo of a bygone era, showcased Robert Young as the proud father, a well-respected doctor (of course). He could work out any family crisis in just thirty minutes (with a few commercial interruptions). He held the wisdom, the power, the glory, and the car keys. His children obeyed him. The family (especially Father) all agreed that Father did know best. Mother was ladylike and quietly concerned. From behind the scenes, she kept the happy household humming. Does this sound familiar?

Back in real life, when we were little, our parents did indeed know more than we did. Often they did know best. Certainly they had all the power and most of the knowledge, and mostly we listened to them. But that was a long time ago, and their script, like the old TV series, is now outdated. Today we know more about ourselves than our parents know about us. We might even be older now than our parents were when they were busy teaching us everything they knew.

It's useful to look again at old scripts and inherited ways of doing things.

Once upon a time

Eleanor's grandmother always cut off the end of the ham before she baked it for dinner. Eleanor's mother and aunts did the same thing. One Christmas morning, Eleanor was about to guillotine the Christmas ham, as the women in her family always had. As she was sharpening the knife, it occurred to her that this was a very peculiar thing to be doing. She was wasting a lot of good meat, because the women in her family always had.

She asked her mother, "Why does our family always hack off the end of the ham before we bake it?" Mother didn't know. The aunts didn't know. No one had ever asked that question. It was just the way they'd always done it. When grandmother came to dinner, they asked her where the tradition came from and why had she always cut the end off the ham. "Because the hams we had on the farm were always too big for my baking pan. So I always cut off one end," she told them. Family traditions usually made sense once upon a time. Generations later, they may not make any sense at all.

Most of our parents wanted our lives to be better and easier than theirs had been, and they worked hard to accomplish these worthy goals. They did unto us pretty much as their parents had done unto them. Knowing they weren't parented perfectly (and who was?), they sometimes tried to rewrite and revise the script they were handed. When we arrived, all new and shiny, their best-guess version of parenting was ready and waiting for us.

We are all just characters in our families' long-running intergenerational series. Some of us never moved on to our own life scripts. Sometimes we feel that we're living a life we didn't create, write, direct, or produce. We may be stuck in a role we've outgrown and don't want any more. We may be miscast. The plot and the writing may be unimaginative. Sometimes we get stuck fulfilling our parents' ambitions, dreams, and scripts instead of our own.

There's a big payoff in not leaving the family soap opera. We don't have to take total responsibility for our own productions. We can blame others when we go over budget or flop. We can stay angry with our parents. We can get sympathy for being misused and abused. And we can feel taken care of. We get to feel both good and bad. We can even feel good about feeling bad. This can become so confusing that we never know what we really want or find out what's best for us.

Adults who don't want to let go of the apron strings often have parents who cooperate wholeheartedly with them. This ongoing, unspoken, working arrangement makes the parents feel needed and the adult child feel valuable and loved. (For example, say you're thirty-four years old and your mother calls to remind you to be careful, to wear your galoshes in the rain, and to wear your hat in the sun. She feels useful. You feel cared for.) When parental apron strings feel like necessary life-support systems, it's hard to let go and leave home.

When adults do decide to manage and run their own lives, they have much more responsibility and much more fun. They get to choose their own roles, their own cast of characters, their own plots, their own settings, even their own mistakes. They get to decide which costumes to keep, mend, discard, or give to a worthwhile cause. They get to choose what fits who they are now and who they want to be.

In the beginning

Envision a circle with a baby in the middle. How large does the circle need to be for the baby to be safe? A baby's first circle of safety is the size of the womb. As the baby grows, the circle expands to the size of the bassinet, the crib, the playpen, the whole house. Eventually it includes the backyard, the neighborhood, the school, and finally the world. As the child grows, each circle is wider, allowing more freedom, more choices, more opportunities to learn, and more room to stretch and grow. Parents have to decide at every stage how much room to give children, whether to expand or contract the circle.

Well-meaning parents, seeking only to protect their children, may rein them in, may draw an impenetrable circle around them that prevents them from making their own mistakes and learning from natural consequences. Working hard to protect their children from life's hard knocks, they can end up teaching fear and dependence. Paradoxically, the more cautious the child becomes, the more the parents relax, believing they're doing an excellent job.

Picture an eighteen-month-old boy toddling near the warm oven door. The parent says, "Hot!" The child doesn't know this word and so proceeds, chubby little hands outstretched, toward the stove. Knowing he won't get burned, the parent chooses to let the child touch the door, resisting the urge to rush in and intercept this learning. When the child touches the warm door, he startles and pulls his hand away with a look of surprise. The parent again says, "Hot!" The child repeats the word he can now understand in a whole new way. Good parenting invents and allows safe ways for children to learn about the world's complexities.

As children's worlds broaden and enlarge, they create their own life scripts. Sometimes their explorations, desires, and visions of the future are punished, criticized, ignored, or denied. Then children become unable to trust themselves. They learn to judge and disown their own dreams and experiences. They may find it hard to hope, dream, or think magically about what they want. Without support for imagining and learning by doing, the child may one day sacrifice autonomy for acceptance and choose safety over freedom. Excessive protection can become a trap, no matter how well intentioned, comfortable, or tender.

Breaking out of the tender (or thorny) trap of childhood usually happens during adolescence. That's the time most of us learned how to say no, break the rules, make new rules, and deal with the consequences. Sometimes the lessons were really harsh. Barry got his first traffic ticket at thirteen when he ran a stop sign on his bike. By eighteen, Paula had learned everything about alcohol. Jeremy shared needles with his high school friends; now he's HIV-positive. We weren't completely protected by our parents. And the painful truth is that we can't completely protect our own children.

In the present

As an adult, if you still feel like a teenager living inside a parental circle, you may feel that you missed something. You did. You may have lost some years along the way. Maybe some muscles never got tried or tested. You may never have gotten angry or rebelled against the status quo.

You may never have acknowledged your separation or budding independence. You may still be acting someone else's script.

It's never too late to begin moving into adulthood, writing our own scripts. We can probably do it now with more tact and grace than any teenager dreamed of. We no longer need to shock, shout, or shake the world in order to rebel. We can stay in dialogue as we find our own paths. Our parents may moan and groan as we move on to new adventures, but they will recover.

Once upon a time

Marie was an accomplished kindergarten teacher in her late twenties. Her parents generously offered to help her purchase her own home and cosigned the note. Although they lived several hours away, they often came down to help Marie fix up and decorate her house. After all, Marie only had her old apartment furniture left over from her student days and no experience being a homeowner. Each time they arrived, her father would bring his toolbox and her mother would bring a chair, a rug, a painting—something to make Marie's home homier. Her parents were retired, and Marie's house became their new career, their new hobby, their new passion. They talked and shopped and made decisions, always with her best interests at heart. Suddenly, their days felt full again.

Marie watched her beloved, raggedy blue couch get taken away by the Goodwill truck. It was replaced by a flowered beige couch that her mother had chosen. Mother had always been known for her good taste.

With each visit the gifts kept coming. One day Marie woke up, looked around, and thought for a moment she was in her parents' house, in the bedroom she'd grown up in. Her home looked just like her parents' home. It had their style, their colors, their taste, their touch everywhere. Her influence was nowhere to be seen.

Marie felt backed into an outgrown, outdated, familiar role. She'd been grateful for all her parents' help, but she realized she had paid a high price. She'd lost her sense of independence, her individuality, her own style. She felt lovingly painted into a corner. Although she'd left home, she was still under her parents' roof.

It had never before seemed necessary or desirable to define her own boundaries, her separateness, her own space. She'd never needed to say no to her parents' generosity. Now, she didn't want to hurt their feelings or seem ungrateful. She'd had the perfect parents, and it was hard to stop being the perfect child.

Marie realized that to make her new home her own, she'd have to make decisions she'd never made before, leave the comfortable circle of her family, and take responsibility. But she wasn't sure of her own taste. Her house might look funny, weird, unacceptable to her parents. What if things didn't match? What if she made mistakes? Well, what if she did? For the first time, they would be *her* mistakes, and the house, for better or worse, would be *her* house.

Marie decided to use her new house to start discovering who she was as an imperfect adult, rather than a perfect child. She figured out how to tell her parents that she was appreciative of all they'd done and that she was now ready to take over. She wanted the final say in any decisions that affected her and her house. Her living arrangements could no longer be their pet project. She braced herself for their shock and surprise. (It's the shock and surprise all parents feel the first time their children don't come home for Thanksgiving.) They would be dismayed at first, but she was hopeful that they would be able to let go and make an easy transition to other interests and passions. And she would slowly figure out how to create her own space and live in her own home.

Leaving our parents' home, physically and emotionally, means more than leaving the town, the state, or the country. It means living our own lives and allowing our parents to live theirs. If you've been the central character in your parents' script, their buffer, their demilitarized zone, their pet project, you may have helped keep the peace in the family. When you exit, the family has to find new ways to be together and develop a new script.

It's not easy to grow up. It's also not easy to be a parent, to know when to give and when to stop, how much is enough and how much is too much. If you now have children of your own, you're probably amazed to find yourself billed as the parent who's supposed to know best.

Parenting takes lots of flexibility and practice. We're always in rehearsal, as were our parents and theirs before them. All parents are always figuring out how to play their roles as they go along, and no parent ever gets it totally right. Only kids think that parents really know what they're doing. Parents know it's all improvisational theater. We don't win any Emmy awards for this role, but we sure learn a lot, meet lots of challenges, get lots of satisfaction, and merit a lifetime achievement award.

Goal

Update and rewrite your own life script. Keep only those episodes and traditions that still work for you. Create new ones. Don't waste time watching reruns. Be prepared for bloopers. Be your own laugh track. In general, you do know what's best for you. When in doubt, ask three people who know you well, three people you trust. They may or may not include your parents.

Set clear boundaries with the people you love the most (like family and best friends). Set limits that you can adjust as circumstances change. Get comfortable with ever widening circles. Know the difference between boundaries and walls. Walls are solid; boundaries are permeable, flexible, and negotiable.

Stretch yourself

If it's hard for you to say no, practice saying it to the plants, to the pictures on the refrigerator, to the dog, until you find a way that works for you. Expand your repertoire of "no" phrases. Practice saying it many different ways.

"I'd rather not."

"Thanks for asking, but . . . "

"This really isn't a good time for me. . . . "

"Let me think about it; I'll get back to you."

"I don't have time. . . . "

"I'm going to say 'no' to that."

"No, no, a thousand times *no*, and please don't ask again!"

Check your wardrobe. Are you dressing for yourself or to look like the person your parents want you to be? Are you dressing for success? Whose? Step back. Look deeply into your closet. Be honest and discerning about what's hanging there. Get rid of the clothes you've outgrown, worn out, or always hated. Give away the clothes that haven't been right for seventeen years, the outfits you didn't choose for yourself. Exorcise the ghosts. Have a garage sale. Eliminate whatever you inherited that doesn't fit anymore. Keep only the items that really suit you. Celebrate who you are.

If you are a parent, are you like Robert Young, a parent who knows best? Are you domineering, overprotective, clinging, or smothering? Ask yourself what it would be like to have you as a parent. Ask your children. They may perceive you in unexpected and imaginative ways.

Traditional parents never asked for or listened to feedback from their kids. You can ask each of your children how you're doing as a parent. Ask if there's anything they'd like you to do differently. Be brave and ask, while your kids are still smaller than you are.

Affirmations

I can produce and direct my own life.

I really do know what's best for me.

I can listen to others (including parents) and make up my own mind.

I can leave home without guilt.

I can make a decision, learn from it, change my mind, and make a new decision.

I can live with imperfect results.

I am responsible for my own show.

I am replacing *Father Knows Best* with *Real Life*.

I'm a grownup; therefore I am.

7

Everyone Else Knows Best?

Myth

Everyone else knows what's best for me, especially professionals like teachers, therapists, doctors, lawyers, and even car salesmen.

Truth

They don't. If you think professional car salesmen know or want what's best for you, you're in big trouble. They're not in business to do what's best for you. They're in business to do what's best for them, to sell cars and make commissions. Their goals are not your goals.

Most professionals are in business to assist you while they support themselves. Doctors are patients' assistants. Lawyers are clients' advocates. Teachers help learners. They all have some expertise, some insight, some answers, some of the time. Sometimes they don't. Mostly they have lots of training, experience, and their best guesses. The best experts will usually help you find your own answers. Sometimes there are just no answers. In truth, all big decisions, even those that look perfect in hindsight, are made on the basis of incomplete information.

For example, you want to buy a used car. You check car magazines, ask friends, speak to dealers, spend Sundays test driving lemons. Your mechanic checks out the cars that feel okay to you. You compare, agonize, and debate; you ask four people and get four opinions. How can you ever be totally sure that your decision is the best one? Isn't there a better car, a lower price, a sweeter deal just around the bend? Perhaps. The one you finally buy may run for two days, two months, two years, or two decades. It's a gamble. You can never really know for sure. You can only know that you made the best guess at that moment in time based on the best available information, and that one day you'll have to go through the process all over again. Alas, there's never a written guarantee that any car, or any decision, will be perfect.

In the beginning

When we were little, we needed others to know what was best for us and to make decisions. Adults fed us, kept us dry and warm, took good care of us when we were sick. They knew how to tie shoes, wash hands, cross streets, and do fractions. The big people who ran the show included neighbors, teachers, nurses, coaches, school counselors, clergy, older siblings, and relatives. Together they served as a kind of parental community. They taught us how to do things and how to live in the world. In the best of times and circumstances, they listened to us. They taught us that our dreams, visions, and questions really mattered. As we got older, they appreciated our insights and opinions. They encouraged us to think for ourselves and to make decisions. When they validated our own internal child's wisdom, we felt really smart. We trusted that we also knew something about what was best for us.

In the worst of times, few big people really listened to us. Our internal wisdom was not valued, and we learned not to trust ourselves. We came to believe that we were stupid, or irrational, or inadequate, or childish, or _____ (fill in the blank). We learned not to trust our own senses, or our good sense. We learned to doubt our own judgment, to look outside ourselves for answers, guidance, and solutions.

Sometimes we were punished for coloring outside the lines, inventing our own spelling, making up our own stories. Sometimes teachers told us that we were bad artists, rotten spellers, or bald-faced liars.

"That's the wrong color for the sky."

"You spelled it wrong again! Write it correctly fifty times."

"That story just isn't true! Stand there until you're ready to tell me what really happened."

"You have to do it the way I tell you to."

"What's wrong with you?"

"You're doing it wrong again!"

No wonder other folks seemed more perfect than we were.

Worn out and down, we easily let others take over and learned to trust them more than we trusted ourselves. For instance, a child will notice that Daddy is unsteady, has a lamp shade on his head, and smells stinky. Daddy is acting strangely. The child knows something is weird and unpredictable. How can Mommy keep saying that nothing's wrong? If we're told again and again that Daddy's just fine, we learn to distrust ourselves and our perceptions of reality. We conclude that we are forever dumb and badly in need of an ultimate expert (like Mommy) to know the truth and to tell us what to believe.

In the present

If we've learned as children to mistrust what we know, we may become incredible shrinking adults whenever we meet people in authority or have to make a big decision. We'll tend to get smaller and dumber in the presence of anyone with initials after their names, stars on their shoulders, or even good posture. Before they can say a word, we tell ourselves that we're inept, clumsy, a potato with bumps. No one should trust us with any decision; we never get anything right anyway.

When we transform authorities into all-knowing or judgmental parents, we tell ourselves we're too little to make big or even small decisions. We imagine that others actually know how to do things better than we do. After all, they are the grownups, and we are not. We give them all the power, shrivel in their shadows, and disappear into the woodwork. We forget our own age and size and wisdom. We forget that we really do know a lot about what we want and what's best for us.

It is true that the most knowledgeable authorities know more than we do in their areas of expertise. Nevertheless, with all their knowledge and experience, even they make judgments based on incomplete data and their best guesses. The best authorities will freely admit that.

Once upon a time

Elaine, who managed a candy store, was called to the hospital to be with her dying mother. During rounds that morning, two doctors suggested doing a complicated exploratory procedure on Elaine's mother's gallbladder. Both doctors agreed that it would be the next diagnostic step. The procedure would give them more precise information about her condition. But one doctor seemed less certain than the other that this step was really necessary. He doubted that it would give her mother any more time or more comfort, and it would be painful. He asked Elaine to decide whether to go ahead.

She was given all the odds: "If we perform the procedure, there's a 60 percent chance that her level of discomfort will increase significantly, and a 40 percent chance it will decrease. The procedure will certainly yield more information about her gallbladder. There are possible harmful side effects and certain potential reactions. It's a gamble. How should we proceed? What do you want us to do? It's up to you."

Elaine's eighty-year-old mother had already been in the hospital for many weeks. She couldn't speak, but she could hear. Listening to the doctors debate, she began shaking her head vigorously. She didn't want the procedure. Clearly, she didn't care about any new information. She'd been through enough. She was tired. Elaine wanted to respect her mother's wishes, but she was confused and surprised to see the doctors unsure and struggling, too.

Elaine asked for time and went down to the coffee shop to think. There just didn't seem to be a perfect solution. Maybe the procedure would help. Maybe it would tell the doctors something different. Maybe it would only cause more suffering. This was a serious moment, and Elaine felt called upon to make the perfect choice. She drank two cups of coffee, ate a sweet roll, and still couldn't come up with the right answer. She went upstairs to find the doctor. She asked him to stop charting for a moment and to think with her.

"If this were your mother, would you have this procedure done?" she asked.

He thought for a long while and finally shook his head. "I don't know," he said.

That was his gift to her. His uncertainty allowed her to feel okay about her uncertainty, about being unsure. She made a leap of faith and decided that "No" was the best answer—not a perfect answer, but the best she could do.

"Let's not do the procedure," she said.

"Fine," the doctor replied, accepting her decision.

Elaine relaxed for the first time that day. She had made her choice and knew she could live with the consequences. She went back and told her mother. Her mother pressed her hand, smiled, and nodded her agreement. Sometimes there is no solution that works perfectly for everyone.

Everybody feels unsure and like a child sometimes, no matter how much alphabet soup (M.D., J.D., Ph.D., CEO) comes after their names, or what kind of power or authority they usually wield. Everybody struggles and everybody agonizes over hard decisions. Everybody feels shorter or taller, depending on who's around and what's happening. Everybody makes mistakes, even those who seem most adult, expert, and perfect.

Like Elaine, when we're uncertain, it's our job to gather and sift through the information we get from the experts, to question authority, and to find the best available wisdom. It's always valuable to know what questions to ask. Because we're the only ones who really know our whole story, we have the final guess on what will work for us in each unique situation. Complex decisions are never easy. As they say, there are no easy answers, and no guarantees.

Despite the complexities of programming the VCR and filling out insurance, income tax, or financial aid forms, it's helpful to remember that we did graduate from the fourth grade. We really are smarter than the average armadillo. We can and must value our own resources, speak out in our own best interests, and call on the experts when it's appropriate. Otherwise we will be shrink-wrapped into being fourth-graders forever.

Goal

Trust yourself. You are the world's foremost authority on your own thoughts, feelings, wants, and needs. You've lived with yourself for a very long time. You know your own history most intimately.

Listen to yourself. Listen to your body. If you get a stomachache every time you have to call Uncle Fred, pay attention. Don't take an antacid right away. Find another way to stay in touch or get out of touch with Uncle Fred. Your stomach knows more than you think it does. Respect its wisdom.

Trust your instincts. Find the balance between what you want and what others know.

Question authority.

Don't be afraid of the imperfect decision. All decisions are imperfect.

Perhaps there are no mistakes, only wrong expectations. Think about it.

Ancient Eastern wisdom suggests: Don't sweat the small stuff; there is no big stuff.

Stretch yourself

Shhhh . . . Practice being quiet enough to hear your wise inner voice, the one that tells you how much you already know. It is your conscience, your stomach, your friend, your guardian angel, the conglomerate of all the best wisdom you've ever heard, thought, or dreamed. To find that inner voice, turn off the noise, slow down, let yourself settle, and listen with respect.

Keep a journal. Print can give your thoughts and feelings a certain authority and respectability and remind you how much you know.

Write down a question using your usual writing hand and use your nondominant hand to write an answer. Dialogue back and forth, shifting from hand to hand. This exercise really works.

Talk to a friend who knows how to listen to you without offering advice, so that you can find your own answers.

Ask yourself a question before you sleep, then sleep on it. Pay attention to your dreams. They are full of good information from your inner world.

Imagine how you would help your best friend if he or she had the problem you're wrestling with.

Here are six helpful questions to aid decision making.

What am I feeling?

What's making me feel this way?

What do I want?

What could I do?

What will be the consequences?

What will I do?

Affirmations

I can listen to and trust my own wisdom.

I give my inner voice as much power as any outer voice.

I know more than I think I do.

The wisest part of me is smarter than I am.

I choose whose advice to take.

I don't have to listen to anybody.

If three people tell me I'm drunk, I will listen and lie down.

I am as grown up as any other adult.

I can listen to suggestions and advice, decide what's useful, and
discard the rest.

I am an unshrinkable person.

I can play in the big leagues.

I decide; therefore I am.

8

Mommy and Daddy
Are to Blame?

Myth

My parents are totally responsible for the mess I am and
the mess I'm in. I was fully formed and fixed by age six.
Now I'm stuck, and they are to blame.

Truth

You are not stuck. No matter how bad your upbringing, no matter what
Freud said, you can unstick yourself and change. You are the sum total
of everything that's ever happened to you—your genes, hormones, siblings, neighborhood, schools, astrological signs, and a thousand other
influences that have no names. The big picture includes the world
beyond parents and family.

Many of us are children or grandchildren of immigrant parents,
people who survived the Great Depression, World War II, the cold
war, the wars in Korea and Vietnam. We were all shaped by the big
realities of geography, culture, historical events, and economics. They

impacted our families in ways we probably knew nothing about. Education, job changes, money problems, relocations, pregnancies, the draft, illnesses—all these were going on in our parents' world while we were busy figuring out how to grow up.

Kids often distort external events, and those distorted memories can have power in our grown-up lives. Little Jeannie's fear of gorillas at the zoo stemmed from hearing the news about guerrillas making war in Vietnam. Johnny felt abandoned when Dad was drafted to fight in a war, while his older brother Mark was proud of his dad for being a soldier. Roger's father was a fireman and his older brother Bill became a fireman, but all his life Roger was frightened by any loud alarm and terrified of fire. Marsha was excited when Mom went to the hospital to have the new baby, but Jackie felt displaced and jealous.

Whatever the event or decision, children interpret and distort it according to their age, their position and role in the family, the stories they are told, and the stories they invent. Growing up is unpredictable. Childhood is very complicated. No single factor, person, or circumstance made us who we were or makes us who we are now. Childhood happened. It's over.

Before your childhood, before the beginning, long long ago, even our parents were little children. They were probably just as innocent and adorable as we were, and they had to grow up under the influence of their own imperfect parents. It's hard to imagine, but there was even a time when our parents were untroubled, loving, and full of life and enthusiasm. They received the imprints of our grandparents, struggled with their particular DNA, inherited their cultural and religious perspectives, and got on-the-job training in parenting. Consider the source. All our ancestors, back to the very beginning of their time in the garden, passed on what they knew about life. Now it's our turn.

In the beginning

We all began life as innocent and adorable babies, and we never had all our needs met. At times we all felt unfulfilled, disappointed, frustrated, angry, hurt, sad, or confused. We were raised not by wolves, but by imperfect human beings in an imperfect world.

It wasn't Eden, but our childhoods were not totally joyless, dreary, and empty. We also got rations of pleasure, excitement, support, tenderness, and compassion. We wouldn't have survived till now if we hadn't.

But alas, some very terrible things did happen to some very good children. If you were treated badly as a child, your only crime may have been to be born either a boy or a girl. Maybe your family was unable to cope with your needy, hungry, demanding, curious, smart, sexual, truthful, loving, human, and imperfect being. If you were punished for any of these normal childhood attributes, your folks were reacting out of their own limitations. They couldn't accept the new challenges that you presented.

It was truly awful if you were hurt, neglected, mistreated, abused, or violated. You should never have been required to take the brunt of anyone else's pain, frustration, misinformation, ignorance, or anger. You were just a child and deserved to be unconditionally loved and encouraged to become strong, loving, and joyful.

Unfortunately, too few of us grew up in that perfect paradise for children. Too few parents, grandparents, foster parents, or stepparents grew up in a paradise for children. We were all expelled from the garden too soon. It's amazing that so many of us do as well as we do, have as much as we have, and give as much as we give.

In truth, many of us had good-enough childhoods, not perfect, not splendid, but good enough. A good-enough childhood included being adequately fed and watered, clothed, occasionally loved, and cared for when we were sick. Most of us were probably taught to ride a bike, catch a ball, or fish. Many of us were encouraged, helped with our homework, praised intermittently, read bedtime stories, or given similar perks. It's all too easy to focus only on the holes and failures of our childhoods. It's harder to remember that we also had some good or possibly great moments and successes and lots of times when it was just good enough. Like childhood, the glass is half full as well as half empty.

Once upon a time

Sue's dad was gone during most of her childhood. He was in the Marines, stationed overseas for years at a time. His leaves from the service were so short and erratic that he always remained a stranger she didn't know or trust. Having an absentee father caused Sue enormous sadness and resentment. By the time he retired and came home for good, she was eighteen and just ready to leave for college.

As an adult walking through an art museum one day, Sue was reminded of a painting that had hung on the living-room wall of her childhood home. Her dad had always been the artist in the family. Sue remembered times when she'd said to him, "Daddy, draw me," and he had. It was magic to watch an image of herself appear miraculously on the blank white page. At those times Sue felt really seen by him.

As a child, Sue had always wanted to be an artist. She was too shy to show anyone her work, but she was always secretly drawing and painting. One afternoon, when she was about ten and her dad was home on leave, he said, "Let's paint a picture." They looked through some books together, and he asked her to pick out a design she liked. She found a face by Picasso and they set out to copy it on a large canvas he'd brought home for her. He let her choose the colors and take the lead. They painted the picture together, solving problems, and laughing. Later they proudly hung the painting in the living room. It was a rare and glorious afternoon.

Sue now realized that whatever else he had or had not done, that day her father had affirmed the artist in her. It was a healing memory, one she had almost entirely forgotten. The recollection of painting together didn't erase Sue's childhood pain about missing her father, but when she recalls that afternoon her memories gain some balance. She remembers that sometimes even he was a good-enough father after all.

In the present

It's so comforting to have someone or something to blame for the imperfect lives we lead. Parents are the most convenient blame catchers. After all, they were the big folks in our little lives, and they were responsible for how we were raised. Now we are the big folks in our little lives, and we are responsible for how we live.

Blaming others can be a rewarding habit with so many advantages:

We don't have to take responsibility for our own choices. "If it weren't for my parents I could have been a prima ballerina, a movie star, author of the great American novel, president of the country, a millionaire, happy."

We can spend more time feeling sorry for ourselves than looking for work.

We can feel self-righteous and powerful in our ongoing anger toward our parents.

We can put all of our creative energy into trying to change our parents instead of ourselves.

We can use our connection to them to stay safe and avoid connecting to anyone else.

We can tell ourselves we're still victims who never get what we want or deserve.

We can make our life's work blaming and punishing our parents for disappointing us.

We can stay sad, bitter, and angry children until we die.

It's often easier to stay on the battlefield with our parents than to call a truce, let go, allow ourselves to mourn, and move on. A truce can feel like losing, and nobody wants to feel like a loser. But a truce is only a cease-fire, and nobody loses when they agree that both parties can put down their arms without losing face. We can allow the war to end and the healing to begin. We could make peace.

When we were children, our parents wanted us to be different, to do everything we were told to do—how and when we were told to do it. Now we want them to be different, to love us, to be sorry, to accept us, to apologize, to do it our way. If we lived in a really perfect world (listen for soft sounds of violins and heavenly choirs), our parents would lovingly come to us, peace treaties in hand. They'd admit all the mistakes they ever made and beg our forgiveness for any and all wrongs. Then we would all laugh and cry together in perfect harmony, understanding, and love. Ah, such sweet music. We would all recognize that the past can't be undone, that we all have regrets, and that we're all going to die one day. We might as well get along. Then we could sign the peace treaty, hire an orchestra, dance, and celebrate until dawn.

Like it or not, the imperfect world we inhabit rarely includes this heavenly scenario. Our childhoods were different for our parents than they were for us. Our memories are rarely their memories. Our agendas were and are different from theirs. We may still be doing battle; they probably thought the war was over when we left home.

We cannot change the past. We can only change how we interpret

63

and feel about the past. We have no power to change our parents. We can only change our responses to them. At best, we might all be able to come together as adults, with mutual respect and good will. We could listen and learn from each other without blame or guilt, without trying to change one another. And the results would be less than perfect.

Richard Alpert, called Ram Dass, is a well-known speaker, scholar, and teacher of meditation. He tells a story about visiting his elderly father for a week and trying to get him to understand and validate his deep commitment to Eastern religious practice. He wore his monk's robes as he lectured and preached to his father, which deeply offending him. One day he decided to let go, just being there with his father instead of trying to convert or change him. He remembered that his father enjoyed playing Yahtzee, so they played Yahtzee often during the rest of the week. They came together in sweet and unexpected ways. In the end, the old man didn't have to validate his son after all.

Goal

Identify your childhood hurts and losses. Acknowledge your truth. Get angry, grieve, forgive, and move on toward an easy acceptance of your flawed childhood and imperfect adulthood.

Practice being a grownup. Grownups don't spend a lifetime (or even twenty minutes) waiting for other grownups (like parents) to change, to apologize, to love them just the way they are, to approve of them, to be like them.

Grownups do unto themselves as they wish their parents had done unto them. You could consider doing unto your parents as you wish they had done unto you.

Grownups recognize that their parents have values that may match or clash with their own. It's okay to grow up and be different.

Grownups take good care of themselves, no matter what kind of care they received as children.

Grownups may not forget, but they can forgive and get on with their lives.

Grownups figure out how to be and not to be with their parents. They can tolerate messy and incomplete endings.

Stretch yourself

Each of our childhood wounds could be seen as a rock that we carry in a sack as we journey through life. Too many rocks can make a very heavy load, one that makes it hard to walk, let alone dance. The goal is to keep emptying that sack as we travel, making room for the new rocks that will inevitably come. Here are some tactics for lightening your load.

Walk a mile in your parents' shoes. Try on one pair at a time. Imagine yourself slipping into the shoes they wore when you were born. As the parent, ask yourself: What are my struggles? What are my passions? My fears? My priorities? How do I feel about being a new and imperfect parent? How do I feel about having you as my child? Repeat these questions as you try on the shoes they wore when you first went to school, became an adolescent, left home. What shoes are they wearing today?

Appreciate and respect yourself as a survivor of your childhood. Honor the qualities that helped you through the bad times—your sense of humor, your passion, your courage, your intelligence, your spiritual beliefs, your patience, your good sense. Ask friends to help lengthen this list. Honor whatever and whoever helped you through the bad times. Include pets, toys, books, siblings, neighbors, teachers, friends.

List the positive qualities you have now because of your wounded childhood—strength, intuition, cleverness, tactfulness, independence, empathy for others.

Get with people you trust, and name the truth of your childhood. Share your war stories. Naming is not blaming. Blaming keeps you tied to the people who did you wrong. Naming, getting angry, grieving what you didn't get, and then finishing will help untie the knots that keep you bound to your childhood. Listen to others. You are not alone.

Identify the types of childhood wounds you received. Were they physical, emotional, mental, spiritual? What scars did they leave in your mind, in your heart, on your body, in your soul? These old war wounds may ache when it rains, or on certain anniversaries, or when they're touched by you or someone else. When you identify the types of wounds you received, you can identify the types of healing that you need. An emotional wound needs to heal emotionally. Spiritual wounds need to heal spiritually. There's no sense in using a Band-Aid when you need a confessional. Heal in the ways that work for you.

Write a letter to each parent. Acknowledge how you're like them and how you're different. Tell them what they did when you were a child, how it made you feel, how it affected your life, and what you want from them now. Do not mail it! Save your letter. Add to it. Revise as needed. When you're ready, burn it.

If you still long for your childhood to be different, create a new one. Invent it. Envision it. Exaggerate it. Turn it into a novel, a farce, a satire, a sitcom. Enjoy.

Adopt surrogate parents. Let them love you.

Be a fabulous parent to your internal child, and to all children. We redeem our own upbringing by doing it better than our parents ever could.

Be careful how you judge your parents. Over the years we all look, sound, and act more and more like them, although we probably swore that would never happen. Like it or not, we are like them. We are also not like them. As adults, we can choose which qualities to keep, which to let go, and which to pass on to our own children.

Affirmations

I can let go of my static clinging to the past.

I am now responsible for the messes I make and the life I live.

My parents are responsible for the messes they make and the lives they live.

I'm okay, even if my childhood wasn't.

My self-worth does not depend on my parents' approval or disapproval.

I celebrate being a grownup.

I'd rather be skiing, flying, in Cleveland, making love, telling jokes _____ (fill in the blank), than blaming my parents.

I survived my childhood; therefore I am.

9

Life Is Fair?

Myth

If I am good and give to people,
they will be equally kind and giving to me.

Truth

Not exactly true. Sometimes, in good faith, we put our quarter in the telephone and nothing happens except we lose our money. Just as telephones will not always be fair, neither will people, no matter how good we are.

We all long for equity, reciprocity, and happy endings. We hate that bad things happen to good people, and bad people triumph. We all want the guy in the white hat to win and Bad Bart to be run out of town. But alas, Bad Bart frequently becomes the governor and the good guy is struck by lightning and dies. Being good doesn't protect anyone from being struck down.

In the beginning

Some of us got lucky. The stork dropped us on the roofs of houses where the folks inside felt abundant, no matter how much they owned. Others of us were left on the roofs of folks who felt impoverished, even if the roof was made of gold. In both kinds of families, as soon as we dropped down the chimney, we learned about giving and getting. Abundant families believed there was plenty for everyone. There was a lot of sharing, a generosity of spirit, and a sense that there would always be enough. Families in which scarcity ruled believed there was never enough. They feared that whatever they had could easily be lost or taken away. They were afraid and taught us to be watchful and to keep score. Sometimes there just wasn't enough to go around. Some families sent the message that the world is both abundant and scarce. No wonder we're confused about when to give and when to receive.

Giving without expecting something in return happens most often when we feel abundant. Feeling we have plenty of love, time, money, wisdom, chicken soup, or zucchinis makes giving easy. Feeling we have scarce resources, we may be afraid to give, not trusting that there will ever be enough. We come to feel as though our survival depends on holding on or being paid back. When we feel frightened our giving, no matter how generous, will have a hook attached. We'll be forever fishing for payback, dividends, appreciation, and be bitterly disappointed when we come up empty-handed. ("After all I did for you . . . ")

In some families, where the rule was "Give or be punished," children learned that they had to give whether they wanted to or not. They grew up in fear of the dreaded S-word. A Selfish child (and we were all Selfish) was seen as unloving, uncooperative, bad, even criminal. Families who didn't distinguish between selfishness and self-care shamed and blamed their children for acting in their own self-interest. Self-care means that we care for ourselves as well as we care for anyone else, that we are one of the people we take care of. Most of us spend a lifetime sorting out how to give to ourselves and to others. We struggle to differentiate between selfishness and self-care.

As kids we all had a great love of fairness and wanted giving and getting to be balanced and just. Some families fostered these values. For example, if a kid cut pieces of cake for herself and her friend, the friend chose her piece first and the kid took the other piece. A kid could watch his favorite TV program for half an hour and then his brothers or sisters took turns watching their favorite shows. These families downplayed competition and promoted cooperation, sharing, and equity. Sometimes kids grow up angry and sorely disappointed that the world doesn't operate the same way their families did.

Some families were not fair. They had favorites, scapegoats, good kids and bad kids. Rules were not equal, balanced, or the same for everybody. No matter whether a family was fair or unfair, some kids grew up bitter and expected the worst. Others became crusaders for social justice and fair play.

In the present

In any relationship, if things are badly skewed in the give-and-take department, hurricanes and tornadoes are inevitable. Storm cellars and lightning rods are advisable. We all need to feel some reciprocity with those closest to us, and over the long term we usually get it. But the demand for perfect parity can be a natural disaster.

Some people keep precise scores and tally up who did what when, who got what when, who did more, and who deserves better. They become so focused on balancing the books to the last penny that they lose sight of the relationship's real value. Relationships are more than checking accounts. Besides, the debits and credits will vary from month to month. It's important to become comfortable with the ups and downs of the balance sheet. Sometimes we give a little more than we get; sometimes we get a little more than we give. People in successful long-term relationships report that they always try to give more than they get and they like doing it that way.

The Golden Rule "Do unto others as you would have others do unto you" says nothing about paybacks, dividends, or capital gains. It reminds us to do for others as we would like done for us, to put ourselves in the shoes of those who will receive what we have to give.

Once upon a time

Tight-lipped Aunt Lucy, the martyr of the family, smiled as she brought soup to the neighbors she despised. Then she complained bitterly that they didn't appreciate all her efforts or her tasty cooking. Martyrs give and give and never get enough in return. The martyr says, "Poor me. . . . After all I did for you . . . " Aunt Lucy pretends she has no choice. She says, "I try and try to do the right thing, and look what happens. No one understands. . . ." She loves to feel like a victim, bathe in the sympathy of others, be righteously indignant, miss out on all the fun. No one around her gets to have any fun, either. We could spend our lives being bitter and disappointed, a party pooper just like Aunt Lucy. But there really are more entertaining options.

Often we shower others with love and attention, cards, and boxes of candied fruit when that's just exactly what we secretly long for. When we give away what we really want for ourselves, we can feel undernourished and grumpy, and look a lot like Aunt Lucy.

However, we can do what Aunt Lucy never did. We can give ourselves more of the good stuff and remind others that even we, the most generous and abundant folks, have needs. The new golden rule is "Do unto yourself as generously as you do unto others." This self-care will significantly decrease the martyr population.

If it doesn't feel right anymore to give until it hurts, stop. It's not easy to change patterns, but you can make new choices when the old ones no longer work. Giving should be a pleasure. It should make you smile. Giving could even give you joy. If you expect nothing in return, you'll never be disappointed.

Think of giving and getting as a spiral, not as a closed circle. Someone gives to you and you give to someone else, not necessarily the same person. Share your abundance somewhere. Trust that the receiver of your gift will pass it on to someone, sometime.

Once upon a time

When Pauline fell off the stair stepper in her exercise class, she broke the fall with her hand and fractured her arm. She was in a lot of pain. Her friend Jack took her to the emergency room and waited while she was X-rayed, bandaged, and given a painkiller. Pauline said, "You go on. I can take a taxi home. You've done enough."

Jack smiled. "I'm happy to take you home. I called in to work; they know I'll be late. I'll get the car."

"But how will I ever repay you?"

"I don't know," Jack said, "but someday someone else at the gym will probably need a trip to the emergency room. And then it'll be your turn."

Take what's given. Say thank you. Pass it on.

Unfortunately, sometimes you will give and give and give and get nothing back. Ever. You will support your wife through medical school and she will run off with the radiologist. You will work for the corporation for twenty-three years and they will let you go the week before your retirement benefits begin. Bad things will happen to good people, no matter how much they give. It's everyone's experience.

Goal

Be good, fair, and generous just because that's who you are. Expect no rewards from other people or the universe. Your generosity to others may or may not be returned. Your generosity to yourself and your own pleasure in giving are the only gifts you can count on.

Move through the world with trust rather than mistrust. Be judicious. Old Eastern wisdom advises you to trust Allah and tie up your camel. Old Western wisdom tells you to expect the best and be prepared for the worst. We think you would be wise to allow for surprises. When you're being a good guy, wear a white hat and carry a lightning rod.

Stretch yourself

You can make the world a better place just by being in it, despite what your parents may have told you. Practice random kindness. Pay the toll for the car behind you. Let someone ahead of you in the checkout line. Buy an extra bag of food for someone who needs it. Offer your services. Read a book to a child. Applaud your mailman, bus driver, car mechanic, local Girl Scout. Smile, pay compliments, be appreciative, offer encouragement. Everybody needs more cheerleaders.

Be one of the people you give to on a regular basis. Give yourself a present every time you give one to someone else—a compliment, a bubble bath, a giggle, a deposit in the piggy bank, a nap, time to read, a walk outdoors.

When you give, your sense of balance may require that you receive something in return. Be clear about what you want and ask for it. Avoid hidden agendas or barbed fishhooks. Negotiate your agreement. Be as straightforward with others as you want them to be with you.

Be generous. Give to the earth by recycling, car-pooling, composting, wasting as little as possible. Flea markets and garage sales are opportunities to save money and recycle. Gandhi said, "Live simply that others may simply live." When you finish reading this book, pass it on.

Affirmations

I can choose when to give and when not to give.
I can choose when to receive and when not to receive.
I'm a good person, even when bad things happen to me.
I'm okay, whether you give to me or not.
I can afford to give more than I get.
Life isn't fair, whether I like it or not.
I give and receive; therefore I am.

10

Original Guilt?

Myth

If only I had been a perfect child, my parents would have been happier,
more sober, less abusive, kinder, healthier. If I had been better,
I could have fixed them and made a perfect family.

Truth

Batman, Superman, and Wonder Woman together couldn't accomplish
this little task, and neither could you.

When we were born, our parents were already grown up. We were
little; they were big. We didn't create their problems, histories, or personalities. We were not responsible for their lives or choices. We didn't
make them sad, tipsy, angry, unkind, or unhealthy.

No one, not even a superhero, was ever born powerful enough to
create terrible parents or ideal parents. Parents were fully formed, more
experienced, more educated, and more or less functional when we
arrived. We had nothing to do with who they were. We don't choose
our parents. We win them and they win us from the big DNA lottery
in the sky.

When you were little you may have been expected to feed the cat, rake the leaves, or pick up your toys. Hopefully, you weren't expected to fix the family car, pay the taxes, cure Aunt Mae's flu, or keep Grandpa alive. Those jobs were too complex for children. Making the ideal family is too big a job for a little kid, too.

In the beginning

Not so long ago, society viewed children as little adults, miniature laborers, necessary contributors to the family's resources. But children are not adults. They're not just smaller, they have different needs, feelings, and thought processes. Only fairly recently did society acknowledge this and pass laws to protect children from working full time in mines, mills, fields, and sweatshops.

But kids are still asked to grow up quickly, and many are asked to take on responsibilities that are bigger than they are. Sometimes they're required and expected to be more responsible and more accountable than any child could or should be. Some unlucky children are asked to be substitute parents and take charge of the family. Psychologists call this extreme situation "parentification."

Once upon a time

Ida was the first born daughter in a large family where both parents worked. While still in elementary school, she helped with her four younger siblings. With each new baby, she had less time to herself. She came straight home from school, stopped playing with friends, and dropped out of band practice. It became her responsibility to keep the house and the smaller kids orderly. She was a little mother before she was even an adolescent.

At first, Ida was proud of fulfilling the parental role. But being mama's little helper was not really much fun. The role grew old before she did. The younger kids resented Ida for acting like a parent. "You can't tell me what to do. You're not my mother!" It was a no-win situation, and it was easier to blame Ida than the absent, hard-working parents.

As she got older and grew more competent, Ida was asked to do more and more, to share her room, to cook, to help the younger kids with their homework. Her parents praised her for her helpfulness and homemaking skills, while the other children in the family were commended for their scholarship, their humor, or their home runs. Ida grew up believing that her only value lay in her ability to nurture others.

Ida's parents often came home from work weary and short-tempered. They often snapped at her for the inevitable chaos that comes with having five children in one house. Ida told herself, "If only I could do more, Mom and Dad would be less grumpy, happier, and more available." Ida could help, but she couldn't make things just right. Both parents working created a hole that Ida couldn't fill. No matter how hard she tried, the hole was bigger than she was.

Ida married young, eager to leave that responsibility behind. She decided never to have children of her own. She'd had enough of being a parent to last a lifetime. Now, as an adult, she struggled to find time to let herself be a child.

If you were a parentified child like Ida, placed in the role of the responsible caretaker, you learned a lot about failure, quickly and early in life. None of us could have the skill or the knowledge to run a home or raise a family when we were only eight. Being eight was just being eight. Little kids' shoulders aren't broad enough to carry such heavy burdens.

Too often, kids are scapegoated and made to pay the price for their parents' unhappy choices. Parents can blame their kids for a host of regrets, failures, lost opportunities, and dashed dreams. "If it weren't for you kids, I could have gone to college, made a fortune, been a contender, stayed sober, left your father, left your mother, been happy, _____ (fill in the blank)." When parents don't take responsibility for their own choices, well-being, or fulfillment, a vacuum is created. Kids (like nature) abhor a vacuum and rush in to fill the empty space. Kids think, "They're right. I should be better, smarter, stronger, funnier, prettier, tidier, faster _____ (fill in the blank). I'm not good enough. If I were more perfect, my parents would have no problems." Kids really want their parents to be happy. Then the kids can be happy, too, and everyone can relax.

Many of us thought we were adopted or dropped into the wrong family because our real parents, we believed, would never have expected us to be grown up before our time. If we had landed in the right family, we believed, we would have been allowed to be kids.

Believe it or not, we weren't the cause of, or the cure for, the problems and frustrations in our families, even if they told us we were. Our behavior as children couldn't change our family then, and we can't make a perfect world now. All we can do is notice how those old beliefs keep us feeling responsible for correcting the universe's messes and imperfections.

In the present

We continue to personalize the flaws in the universe. We assume that we alone have done something wrong when our worlds aren't perfect. When we take all the blame and carry all the pain, we are suffering from original guilt. It started so early in our lives, we feel as though we were born with it.

Original guilt tells us that from the beginning we were wrong, undeserving, and unforgivable. We learned it as kids and deep down we still believe it. So we keep trying to prove our worth by fixing everyone and everything. We become the world's mechanics. Even though we couldn't fix our original families, we continue using our toolkits to tinker with everyone different from us. Surely, given all our knowledge about how things ought to be, we should be able to save the spouse, mend the friend, prod the parent, train the teenager, control the cat. We tell ourselves, "If only they would do it our way . . ." They don't.

Some people, like parents, may not want to change, although they may not be living the way we think is best for them or us. They may not be measuring up to our standards. Their lives may look miserable, sad, and lonely to us. But, perhaps they're committed to their own ways of doing things. Maybe they like their lives just as they are. Maybe their ways work for them. Maybe they are who they want to be and how they want to be. Maybe they have family traditions. Maybe they have family curses. Maybe it's their right not to change, and not to have us meddling in their lives.

Original guilt doesn't end when we leave home. It can keep us attached to our parents by an invisible thread a thousand or more miles long. That thread can keep us tangled up in knots, feeling inexplicably

anxious and disloyal whenever we're happier, healthier, or more successful than anyone in our family. We may feel a tug on the thread when
we laugh louder, have more friends, make more money, do better than
our parents did. It may be easy to move away, but it's not so easy to
leave home.

As children, we couldn't change our parents or our siblings. As
adults, we still can't change anyone. But we can influence our world
and make small differences. We need to learn when to butt in, when to
butt out, and when to leave well enough alone. Sometimes change just
happens. Sometimes we can encourage it to happen. Sometimes we
can't. Sometimes we can be helpful. Sometimes we're helpless.
Sometimes helpfulness is no help at all.

Goal

Forgive yourself for not being able to make your family perfect. You
were not born a superhero with magical powers, nor are you ever likely
to be one.

Let go of wanting more for your parents (or anyone) than they
want for themselves.

Quit trying to change others the way you tried to change your parents. Your efforts didn't work then; they won't work now—not with
friends, coworkers, lovers, or mates. Trying to change others is kind of
like teaching cows to sing. Cows just don't want to sing. They like
standing around in fields, chewing, being quiet, mooing occasionally.
They resent and resist anyone who pushes them to be different.

Don't measure yourself by how well the adults or cows close to you
are doing. Their lives are their responsibility. Let go. Your life is your
responsibility. Take hold. Don't let anyone keep you from as much happiness as you can tolerate.

Stretch yourself

Write a letter to the six-year-old who still lives inside you. (What was
your name then?) Write the truth in very specific detail. Tell yourself
what was irreparable in your house and how much power you really had
as a child. Put the responsibility where it belongs. Forgive yourself for

not having reformed the adults in your life. Forgive yourself for having been their child, their scapegoat, their parent. You couldn't stop them from being who they were. They would have been pretty much the same whether you had been born or not.

Make a very long list of all the people in your life who need or needed even a little fixing. Take a deep breath. Fixing other people, no matter how broken, is a thankless task at best. It's not your job. It never was. Maybe you could put your caring and concern to better use by loving and accepting them just as they are. Your life will be easier. So will theirs. Let them be. Tear up the list.

Notice the size of the shoulders on your friendly neighborhood eight-year-olds. How many adult problems would you ask them to carry? How many can you carry, even now?

Affirmations

I was an imperfect child in an imperfect family. Now I'm an imperfect adult.

My parents chose their own lives, and I get to choose mine.

I can be happy, successful, sober, kind, healthy, even if my parents weren't.

I can let go and let my parents be.

I'm not a superhero.

I can care about others without trying to change them.

I can butt in, and I can butt out.

I can try making the imperfect world a better, not a perfect, place.

I can be an excellent parent to myself and to children.

I can take care of myself without feeling guilty or selfish.

My power is limited; therefore I am.

11

Codependents 'R' Us?

Myth

When I help others, I am being hopelessly codependent.

Truth

Not so. *Codependency* has become a negative label applied to genuine helpfulness, generosity, and unselfishness. We all become necessary codependents in times of trouble. We put our own needs aside temporarily to stretch and sacrifice for another, the way parents often do for their young children, the way families often do when one is ill. Our natural inclination is to be helpful, generous, and caring, and goodness knows, the world needs all the help, generosity, and care it can get. No one calls Mother Teresa hopelessly codependent.

Unnecessary codependency means continuing to stretch and sacrifice long after our services are needed or wanted. Unnecessary codependency resembles vitamin-deficient chicken soup. It might nourish a little in the short term, but it keeps the hungry person needing more, and it keeps the cook stuck in the kitchen over a hot stove. Chicken soup can be poison when it depletes the drive to get well, and the cook seems to be the only savior, the only rescuer, the only one who really understands, the only resource—the only solution.

Unnecessary codependency is a sincere perversion of love. It can include:
- wanting more for others than they want for themselves
- taking better care of others than we do of ourselves
- taking more responsibility for others than they take for themselves
- giving to others what we really want for ourselves
- keeping others needy by doing for them instead of encouraging them to do for themselves

Healthy codependency means taking care of yourself while you take care of others and setting clear and definite boundaries. It's finding the right balance so that you don't burn out while doing for another, and you don't make the person in need totally dependent on you alone.

In the beginning

Not all that long ago, there was no such word as 'codependence.' The concept comes out of the alcoholic recovery movement and describes a particular set of behaviors. Al-Anon was probably the first to recognize these issues and address their impact on families and children. Alcoholics or other habitually addicted people frequently create unhealthy relationships with their parents or spouses. Such people may function as enablers, or codependents, people who unwittingly foster the addict's behaviors. When the addict is dependent on a mood-altering drug of choice, the enabler takes care of, makes excuses for, and supports the user's habit. Their relationship is called codependent. Even when enablers think they're trying to get the user to sober up or go straight, their behavior keeps things in balance so that the user can go on using.

Sometimes codependent behavior is very blatant; sometimes it's very subtle. Blatant behavior can include calling the boss to make excuses for the hungover drinker, having a cocktail or two to keep the alcoholic company, denying there's a problem when the kids complain about the user's erratic behavior. Subtle codependency includes keeping the family going and covering up no matter what. The user never has to realize that their using is a problem with harsh consequences, that it hurts the people they live with and love the most.

The concept of codependency has expanded to include all types of excessive caretaking and extreme emotional dependence on others. In the middle of a complex relationship it's often hard to sort out who's being sincerely generous and who's being codependent.

Once upon a time

On a cold and frosty night, a kindly and gentle woman found a poisonous snake on the road beside her house. It had been run over by a car and was half frozen and half dead. Tenderly, she picked it up, carried it into the house, warmed it by the fire, and nursed it back to health. One day as she was feeding it a freshly toasted and buttered mouse, the snake suddenly turned and bit her hand.

"Why did you bite me, after all my kindness, after all the care I gave you?" she asked, as she felt the poison spreading through her body.

"Why are you s-s-s-s-so s-s-s-s-surprised?" asked the snake. "You always knew I was a venomous s-s-s-s-snake. You knew that I was-s-s dangerous-s-s-s-s. It is my nature to bite."

The woman lay on the ground trembling. "But I was so good to you. I believed that you wouldn't hurt me, that our relationship would be special, that you would treat me differently."

The snake did not respond. It slithered off into the sunset and left the woman to die.

Codependents forget that people will be true to their nature. Some will bite the hand that feeds them. Codependents live with a false sense of security. They often don't want to be confused with the facts. They don't want to notice the fangs on the folks they take care of.

Codependents are so nice. They do everything for others without explicitly asking for anything. Secretly they long for substantial rewards—engraved "Codependents 'R' Us" trophies for the mantle— but they'll settle for the eternal hope that their partners will change one day and appreciate them at last.

Codependents worry about offending, so they never define boundaries. They never say no, never make waves, never complain. They hate to argue. They're always helpful and willing to do more than their share. They gladly take the blame for everything and are so responsible that they'll stay awake worrying about other people's problems. They rarely notice their manipulations are really to control the other, to see to it that things are done their way. It is said that codependents are so busy living their partner's life that just before they die, their partner's life passes before their eyes.

Some codependents are not too nice. They suffer, nag, and whine about not having a life of their own. No one thanks them enough for their pain and martyrdom. They feel like forgotten victims who rescue but never get rescued. Such codependents are committed to being righteous and indispensable. They feel resentful because nothing and no one around them is changing and everyone else is having more fun than they are.

All codependents begin by trying valiantly to make things work. They progress from doing what's helpful to taking on too much and hanging in too long. They move along a continuum that ranges from most compassionate and generous to most controlling and narcissistic.

Codependency often begins in families where kids aren't allowed to grow up. Overzealous parents are unwilling to cut the umbilical cord or untie the apron strings. They give kids much more help than is needed, force feeding advice, assistance, and attention. They carry their grown kids around as if they were still children, even when their kids outweigh them. They never feel okay about letting their old, grey, and experienced children make decisions. In order to stay parents forever, they need to keep their children needy and close to home.

Codependency thrives where children are trained and rewarded for taking on everyone's needs but their own. Traditionally, girls were groomed to become super little helpers and selected for intensive codependency training. This was deemed necessary for future wives and mothers.

Today anyone can become a student at Codependency U, taking courses in Self-Denial 101, Introduction to Tenacity 102, Living with Pain 301, Total Availability 302, Rescuing 402, Advanced Martyrdom 403. Graduates are celebrated far and wide for being caretaking heroes. They carry on their frail but willing shoulders the problems of anyone bigger or smaller than they are. The big C on their well-padded sweatshirts stands for "Count on Me!" "Can Do!" "Completely Capable Caretaker!"

In the present

Alumni of Codependency U do not laugh. They take themselves very seriously. These are some of the statements they say to themselves in the dark of night or to others in the heat of day. Codependents believe them, and live their lives making them come true.

1. If I am good enough to you, you will want to stop drinking, doping, raging, being unfaithful. Until then, your habit is my problem and my obsession.
2. You are the problem; I am the only solution. You can't possibly make it without me.
3. I am the good guy—noble, generous, and honorable. I do for you whether you want me to or not. You are the bad guy.
4. What began as a little nurturing has become my life's work. Now I feel most nourished when I am most depleted by your needs.
5. I am forever your parent. You are forever my child. I always know what's best for you. Even when I am dead, I will still haunt you as your best and most critical parent.
6. Your well-being is my career. If you get well, I will be unemployed. I'll have to find someone else's life to manage.
7. I am indispensable. After all I have done for you, you must stay with me forever.
8. You can never repay what you owe me. I will remind you of your indebtedness every day of your life.
9. I will never reject you so you will never reject me.
10. You should be doing unto me what I am doing unto you.
11. When something's not being done, I react and jump right in to fix it. I can't tolerate anything being out of control, or anyone else taking over.

Once upon a time

George's elderly grandfather caught pneumonia and was hospitalized for two weeks. George took it upon himself to watch over his aging grandmother. She was still spry and competent and had lived a balanced, loving life with her husband for forty-seven years. George, a closet codependent, took on his new responsibility with verve and gusto, never asking how he could be most helpful. He stopped at his grandmother's house every morning before work. He called three or four times during the day. He rushed home from work to take her to the hospital, although she was perfectly happy to drive herself. He cooked dinner for her, even though she was happy to cook. He felt terrific. She felt smothered.

After a week of being hovered over and treated like a needy and inept three-year-old, grandma told George that she appreciated his concern but he was making her into a dependent old lady. She asked him to please leave her alone except when she asked for something. George was crushed. During his week as her caretaker he had felt needed, useful, generous, and great-hearted. He tried to convince her that she couldn't get on without him, but he failed. Fortunately, Grandma was sharp and clear and knew what was happening. George was lucky. Some folks would have taken everything George had to offer and then some.

It took George more than a day to understand that Grandma didn't need to be dependent on him. He needed to be needed and was shocked when she sent him away. He was becoming dependent on her and blind to her strengths. He realized that he was really lonely and longing for connection, and he needed to find other outlets for his generosity and desire to nurture. It would be too easy to become a lifetime codependent in search of a willing victim.

As with George and Granny, codependency can progress from simple acts of generosity to a complex of controlling relationships and self-defeating caretaking. It's often hard to notice when we cross the line from simple giving to complicated codependency. Fortunately George moved on, unlike many codependents who hang on to a frozen vision of how their relationships should be. Like children, they're often possessive, jealous, and afraid to let go. Like overzealous parents, they worry that if they relax even a little, the relationship will change. They're right.

People in the helping professions need to be especially sensitive to signs of creeping codependency. Social workers, teachers, counselors, nurses, nannies, day-care workers, and homemakers are all generally underpaid and overworked. They are especially vulnerable to burnout.

All caregivers need to watch out for anger and resentment, fatigue and depression. Truly caring people need to be cared for, too.

Some alumni of Codependency U went to graduate school, where they questioned and unlearned their early codependency training. They do what's needed while taking care of themselves. They move out of their familiar comfort zones and respond (sometimes heroically) to unexpected situations. They are able to behave as adults and expect and allow others to do the same. They know how to love and set limits. They meet life's challenges and do the best they can under the circumstances. They recognize that we are all interdependent. We need to give and get a lot of help along the way.

All of us are codependent at times; we all long for healthy relationships. Healthy relationships can be fun. Except on rare occasions, they don't hurt. They're not always in crisis and don't cause undue stress or ulcers. Partners accept that sometimes each person will need to be especially caring or cared for. They don't try to fix one another. They're considerate, respectful, and loving. They don't expect life or the other person to be perfect. They don't blame. Like adults, they take responsibility for their own actions and are open to new experiences, new friends, new ways of doing things. They foster each person's uniqueness, creativity, and growth. They change and adapt to new situations. They work it out together. They're trusting. Separateness and aloneness are allowed and respected. They're interdependent. They talk. They listen. They laugh.

Goal

Question the notion of codependence. Distinguish necessary from unnecessary codependency. Don't let the labels stop you from being kind and generous.

Notice your own style of giving. Experiment with new and imaginative ways to give or not to give.

Continue to help others. Maintain and deepen compassion. Do service. Honor loving kindness in yourself and others. Stay connected to your own needs.

To avoid dangerous codependency, practice the following rules:

Don't give until it hurts unless absolutely necessary.

Define your boundaries and bottom lines.

Don't take in any poisonous s-s-snakes.

Don't work harder than everyone else.

Let go of changing anyone else.

Make relationships with people who don't need you to fix them.

Don't ever suffer any more than you have to.

Search for and celebrate healthy relationships and interdependence.

Stretch yourself

If you've been the perfect codependent, stop. "Just say no." This will frustrate and surprise your children, your partners, your friends. Benign neglect can be good for them; it can foster independence, self-sufficiency, and creativity.

Notice whether you are remaining a child to keep your parents or partners occupied and fulfilled doing the age-old work of helping you grow up. Notice this especially if you are over thirty. Surprise and disappoint everyone. Grow up.

Helpful hints:

1. Back off. Don't always be in the middle, arranging everything. Share the middle.

2. Whenever you do something for someone else, do something for yourself.

3. Never allow anyone to physically or verbally abuse you.

4. Don't think alone. Call in other resources.

5. Get someone to rub your shoulders. Feel their true size. Realistically, how much can you carry at this time in your life?

6. Ask yourself, "Whose problem is this really? Who really needs to make changes?"

7. Look at your job description. Your job doesn't include rescuing anyone from their irresponsible behavior.

8. Set clear boundaries. Be calm. Say what you mean and mean what you say.

9. Don't lie to yourself or anyone else. Don't let anyone lie to you.
10. Don't finance or support anyone's addiction.
11. Don't let anyone spoil your day. Life is too short.
12. Continue finding new ways to feel needed, important, indispensable, and vital.

Affirmations

I can give a lot and not be codependent.

I call a s-s-snake a s-s-snake. I don't expect miracles.

I take care of myself as well as I take care of you.

I can give to myself what I've been giving away.

I can be independent and allow you to be independent of me.

I can choose to be interdependent.

I can choose to be or not to be codependent.

I give and take; therefore I am.

12

Controlling the Entire Universe?

Myth

I must always be in control of my entire universe
or terrible things will happen.

Truth

You're not in control of your universe. You never were. You never will
be. No one is. No one will be. Forget it. You're barely in control of your
own alarm clock. Life is messy and so is the universe. Comets collide,
fruit rots, arches fall. Not only are you not in control, but you can quit
looking for someone who is.

Life is not a spic-and-span supermarket; it's more like a flea market—wonderfully untidy, unfinished, unresolved, and imperfect. It's full
of messy, ragged beginnings and endings. It's out of control.

In the beginning

If you were a perfect child and had the perfect childhood, you must have had perfect parents. If you are a PACOPP, a Perfect Adult Child Of Perfect Parents, you undoubtedly have some illusions about control. They are left over from a world long, long ago, and far, far away when you were very young.

Like all toddlers, you probably made up your own rules about control. The toddler property laws are nearly universal.

1. If I like it, it's mine.
2. If it's in my hand, it's mine.
3. If I can take it from you, it's mine.
4. If I had it a little while ago, it's mine.
5. If it's mine, it must never appear to be yours in any way.
6. If I'm doing or building something, all the pieces are mine.
7. If it looks just like mine, it's mine.
8. If I saw it first, it's mine.
9. If you're playing with something and you put it down, it automatically becomes mine.
10. If it's broken, it's yours.

The big disappointments of growing up include finding out that everything isn't yours, that there is no Santa Claus, and that you are not in charge of the cosmos. This last disappointment can also be a great relief. You were not responsible for all the great things or all the terrible things that happened then, and you're not responsible now. Things happened, great and terrible, and you were just a kid—an innocent bystander, an unsophisticated, inexperienced, naive participant. You were not the director, producer, or master of the universe.

The illusion that we can control the universe often comes from growing up in a super-structured, controlled environment, a Spotless world, with Mr. and Mrs. Spotless in charge. We all know a Mr. and Mrs. Spotless. They keep a germ-free, sanitized house, which is their pride and joy. Mr. and Mrs. S. take great pride in their immaculate bathrooms and children. There are no footprints on their carpets. They allow no disruptions, nothing unexpected, out of line, or out of place. Everything and everyone around them is sterilized, organized, and deodorized. The sofa has a plastic cover and everything is under control, including the children.

Mr. and Mrs. Spotless feel righteous. They're proud of looking just perfect to the rest of the world. No bugs dare cross their thresholds. No dust bunnies ever germinate under their beds. No wildlife is allowed. Armed with Raid and Lysol, they never relax, nor does anyone around them. The cross-stitched sampler on the wall reads, "Cleanliness is next to Godliness." And, yes, you could eat off the floors if you were so inclined.

Mr. and Mrs. S. have created a thousand ways to micromanage their lives. By exterminating all the little bugs outside, they can avoid being bugged by the creepy crawlies inside their relationships or their psyches. Fanatically controlling dirt and disorder keeps them from noticing whether their marriage is spotty at best, messy as an unmade bed, or stale as yesterday's coffee. They stay hypervigilant, on the alert for nasty imperfections in others, and no one is ever perfect enough, including their children. They can hardly tolerate the world as it is—dirty, messy, untidy, unruly, and alive. So they zealously create a brave new world that's heavenly, spotless, organized, and dead.

Alas, this is not a very brave new world for the Spotless children, who pay a high price for their parents' fears and obsessions. They are meticulously toilet trained. Their fingernails and ears are checked daily, and their bodies are scrubbed hard.

In the Spotless world, where no trial-and-error experiments in learning or mishaps are allowed, kids are not allowed to be kids. They have to grow up very quickly and learn their place in the order of things. They have to trade their messy individuality for the bed on which you can bounce a quarter. "One spot on the dishes and you'll wash them all again." "One dirty word and I'll wash your mouth out with soap." "Mess up this house and you'll be sorry." The Spotless children know they'll be shamed and punished for being disorderly or disobedient, so they, too, become nervous, hypervigilant, and unnaturally clean and critical. They know the unruly, human, and imperfect parts of themselves and others are not tolerated in the Spotless house.

The good news is that it's not so easy to kill off the vitality and spirit of children. They will find places to express their youthful energy and creative ways to subvert all that in-sanitizing control. They'll act out, go slow, get numb, or run wild away from home. They'll often

91

dominate and terrorize younger siblings or pets to feel that they, too, have some power, some control somewhere, over something. You know how it's done; we've all done it.

The opposite of Mr. and Mrs. Spotless, down the street, across the way, living in wild disarray, is the Chaos family. Sometimes their disorder spills out onto the front porch, and sometimes it stays hidden behind closed doors and out of the neighbors' view. At the Chaos house, everyone is home, but no one is really there. No one is in charge. No one is running the ship.

Lost at sea, the Chaos kids long for someone to take charge, to keep things safe, organized, and running smoothly. But for one reason or another, Mr. or Mrs. C. can't seem to clean up their own messes, and they keep creating more. They may be seriously preoccupied, overwhelmed, ill, immature, or addicted to alcohol or other drugs. These adults can barely handle their own lives, their own pain, their own disorder. Managing a family is beyond them. They keep changing the rules, breaking their promises, creating crises. The Chaos family is out of control.

Because someone in a family has to be in charge to keep the ship from going down, the kids will try to take over. They will man the wheel, tug on the sails, swab the decks, keep watch for icebergs, hurricanes, and tidal waves. But families, like ships, are too big and complex for children to sail. And the seven seas are frightening and full of surprises. Loyally standing watch, these little sailor children can become worried and anxious, trying to ward off impending doom, forever rearranging the deck chairs on the Titanic. They do the best they can. Some valiantly get the littler ones off to school, get dinner on the table, get excellent grades. Some abandon ship entirely to play baseball or run with the wind in the vacant lot next door.

Once upon a time

In Patti's chaotic family, her mother, Mrs. C., had been ill, irritable, terribly overweight, and depressed all her adult life. She had never really wanted any of her four children, three boys and one girl. Every day when Patti came home from grade school, she found Mother in bed, depressed, and the breakfast dishes still on the kitchen table. Mother would angrily emerge from her darkened bedroom and direct Patti to clean up breakfast and begin dinner.

Patti was an obedient child and willing to help, but she was forever tossed by her mother's storms, buffeted by angry blasts. Patti tried and tried to do everything right, but the rules kept changing. Mrs. Chaos wanted things first this way, then that way. Because her mother was so angry, Patti assumed she must have done something terribly wrong. Feeling responsible, she tried hard to manage and diminish her mother's unpredictable rages by controlling herself, being perfectly contained, silencing her own voice. Nothing worked. Nothing made sense. No one ever told her that her mother had been out of control long before she was born.

Mired in confusion, Patti longed for some sensible direction, some reasonable way to navigate. She craved peace and freedom and envied her brothers playing in the backyard while she scrubbed the carrots and tried not to get buried at sea. Patti failed to control the uncontrollable forces of her childhood. She grew up fearing and avoiding her own imperfections and any signs of chaos. She created the tightest, tidiest, safest, and most controlled life she could. She fell in love with angry, critical men and soon gave up on messy relationships. They were just too chaotic for the spotless world she needed.

If your family was Spotless or Chaotic, and you were punished for making mistakes, for not managing the irascible grownups in your family, you probably took it personally. Now, as a grownup, you may be like Patti, frightened or overwhelmed by disorder and still struggling to maintain control over yourself, your world, and everyone else's.

In the present

As adults we do have much more power over our lives than we did as children. We now have car keys or bus fare and can leave the Spotless bathroom or the Chaotic kitchen behind. Being grown up means we can make our own rules and our own messes. We can choose to play in the rain, go to bed after nine, eat dessert first, spend the night with folks our parents would have hated. We can also establish some order, some boundaries, some systems to keep ourselves from total chaos and complete disaster.

Taking charge is a many-splendored thing. It is helpful and down-right convenient to have some mastery over our bowels, our tempers, our charge cards, our crabgrass, our time. It's useful to have some order in our checkbooks, our closets, our desks, our days. We get out of control with control only when we try to move from a fairly well-regulated life to a completely structured life. Beyond orderliness, beyond reason, control can become a goal in itself. We can take it to extremes and suffer from the top six extreme delusions.

Extreme Delusion Number One: We can eliminate any disorder in our lives. If we can manage the messes in our kitchens, we should be able to tidy up any messes in our world. Alas, our power is always limited. Unexpected surprises, people, and events change everything in an instant. We can snuggle up to this notion, or we can spend our lives resisting it. We can roll with the punches or keep our jaws and fists clenched, seeing surprise as our opponent, determined to go the full nine rounds. Either way, being really grown up means noticing that we are not in charge of everything.

When we get nervous about the chaos in our lives, the big stuff, we naturally try to calm ourselves and take charge where we can. We find some relief by controlling the small stuff—our hairdos, our sock drawers, our desk tops, our tax files. That's about the best we can do. And sometimes even the small stuff is unpredictable.

Extreme Delusion Number Two: We can totally control all our intimate relationships. We can make someone love us, stay with us, take care of us, do it our way. We can coach them, train them, manage them, take them hostage. We can bonsai our nearest and dearest into tiny little lacquered pots.

Some people can allow relationships to happen spontaneously and evolve gracefully; others have tight expectations and fear anything that just happens and evolves. When controlling others doesn't work, we become frightened. Too often, the more frightened we become, the more tyrannical we become and the more elaborate control tactics we devise, including brainwashing, terrorism, passivity, and mystery.

Brainwashing works. Disapproving, blaming, judging, discouraging, and more blaming will surely encourage guilt, shame, and low self-esteem in our partners. This is the tyranny of negativity.

Terrorism works. Verbal or physical abuse will intimidate others and clarify who's the boss. Threats, isolation, and punishment do encourage fear, self-doubt, and victimization. This is the tyranny of brute force.

Passivity works. Giving others anything they want, being indispensable, and avoiding conflict and disapproval will keep our partners happy, hobbled, guilty, and indebted. This is the tyranny of the good.

Mystery works. Withdrawing, becoming silent, or disappearing makes others sweat, as they wonder what we really want and what they've done wrong. Resisting others sexually, emotionally, or physically can encourage anyone to grovel for a crumb of recognition or validation. This is the tyranny of silence.

Tyranny is very effective and works for the short, and sometimes long, term, and it leaves wreckage everywhere. It can demolish the one who isn't the tyrantasaurus. Tyranny is the mask of fear, the opposite of love. It controls and alienates those we love best.

Extreme Delusion Number Three: We know what's best for everyone around us and need to control them for their own good. Others rarely appreciate how much we worry and how hard we work to manage their lives. They may even see us as control freaks, fussbudgets, nags, or dictators. They probably resent being treated like children, told to clean up their messes, to live their lives as we see fit.

We get into big power struggles when we try to convince other adults to honor, obey, and love our values and rules as much as we do. How insensitive of them not to realize that we only want what's right and best for them. This is a lonely and unappreciated predicament for those who feel obliged to be in charge of everyone.

Extreme Delusion Number Four: We should have absolute mastery over our bodies. We should never have low energy, never get sick or gain weight. No germs or viruses, no sags or creases, no unnecessary bulges or extra pounds allowed. Our bodies should obey our minds.

We do have some control over our appearance and, like Hollywood, can create illusions of youth, of health, of immortality. We can dye our hair, get the face lift, the tummy tuck, the hair transplants, the liposuction. But these things only change the small stuff on the outside. We can't budge the big realities on the inside. We do get sick. Our bodies change. Chemistry shifts. Accidents happen. It's beyond our control. We are only cocreators of our physical well-being. We share responsibility with our genes, our histories, our sensibilities, our immune systems, and Lady Luck.

Most of us are grateful not to be in charge of our spleens or our pituitary glands. It's a pleasure to trust that our lungs and kidneys will do their jobs. Our body has a mind of its own and knows much more about its functions than we do.

Extreme Delusion Number Five: If we were really perfectly in control we would never grow old or die. We would stay young, vigorous, fertile, and strong forever. We would be immortal.

As youngsters, we never imagine being over thirty. Then we wake up one morning, and suddenly we're looking more and more like our parents and grandparents. Our doctors, policemen, politicians, and bosses are suddenly younger than we are. We've aged. It's out of control.

If we don't die first, we will get old. We will be thirty, forty, fifty, sixty-plus, and we will find out that aging has its benefits and surprises. Certainly, it's better than the alternative. Our last years can even be the most liberated part of our lives. We can be free and difficult. Our wrinkles announce that we've been somewhere, that we know something. Our rhythms allow us to slow down and enjoy all the seasons. We will not always be in the springtime of our lives. Autumn happens. So does winter. We will die. It's perfect.

Dying is not about control; it's about being mortal. We can only influence the quality of our lives from now until the end. Satchel Paige said, "If I knew I would live this long, I'd have taken better care of myself." Death is the biggest reminder that nothing lasts forever and we're not in charge.

Extreme Delusion Number Six: I should have godlike powers. I should be able to fix anything that doesn't work—personally, socially, politically, and universally. I should be able to foretell the future, perfectly predict the ups and downs of the stock market, and avoid all failure. This delusion leads to endless frustration, bitterness, and a deep sense of shame.

Control over the universe would probably work best if you were God. Godlike isn't God. Not even close. Let's face it, our individual spark of divine power has severe limitations. When we long for order and feel we must do something, we can only dust off our tiny corner of the planet. We're not superhuman. We have to stand by helplessly and watch the universe spin out of control, creating unsightly black holes, crashing meteors, and shrinking ozone layers. Appreciating that we're only an insignificant speck of cosmic dust in the infinite chaos gets easier with practice.

Extreme Truth: Traditionally, control of the cosmos was divided. God was in charge of the universe. Men were in charge of business, money, and everything else in the dog-eat-dog world. Women were in charge of the house, food, and children in the hectic kid-chase-cat world. Now the divisions are less clear, and no one seems to be entirely in charge of anything.

Goal

Loosen your grip on the controls. When controlling controls you, admit it, if only to yourself, quietly, before sunrise. Then do something about it.

Sort out what you can control, what you can influence, what you can't affect at all, and what's really none of your business.

Rethink your unrealistic expectations. They are a direct road to disappointment, frustration, and anger.

When you're worried about who's in charge, remember what your first-grade teacher said. Learn to share with others. Let them have some control, too. They'll like it.

Notice that the universe functioned pretty well before you were born, and it probably will function pretty well after you're gone—not perfectly, but pretty well. You don't really need to be God. That job is already filled.

Stretch yourself

Make friends with being out of control sometimes. Swim in the ocean. Ride a roller coaster. Let someone else drive. Have an orgasm. Get a cat. Have a kid. Any of these will remind you how little control you really have.

Lighten up. Cultivate play, humor, clowning, banana peels. Enjoy babies and bubbles. Laugh at yourself. There are enough very serious people trying to control the world.

Get dirty. Allow grunge in your life. Tolerate what's natural. Make friends with your mayhem, confusion, and disorder. Take a moment to

appreciate the spontaneous science experiments in the plastic contain-
ers in your refrigerator. Don't panic. Things grow. It's a miracle.

Take a cue from nature, where leaves know when and how to let
go, litter the ground, and transform into compost. The natural world
makes a terrible mess. Walk in the woods—ungroomed, disheveled,
unkempt, undomesticated, wild, shocking.

Accept your God-given limitations. You've got a million of them.
Cherish your stupendous ability to make mistakes, large and small.

Find or make your own patron saints of imperfection: St. Egg-on-
your-face, the saint of missing car keys, the saint of short-term memory
lapses, the saint of missed freeway exits. Put them where you'll see
them every day. They'll remind you that you're doing just fine bum-
bling through your slightly out-of-control life.

Unplug your self-esteem from how well others are doing. All
imperfect kids, partners, parents, coworkers, friends, Romans, country-
men are beyond your control. No need to feel ashamed and inadequate
about the million choices they make in their lives. You're not in charge,
and you don't need to be anguished or critical. They're responsible for
their lives; you're responsible for yours. If you must control something,
organize and dominate something that won't resent you afterwards.

Watch *M*A*S*H* reruns. Hawkeye and the others can do very little
to save the wounded who come into the field hospital. They do their
best, with skill, humor, and courage, but they're not gods and they can't
fix everything. They win some; they lose some. So do we.

The AA people say, "Let go. Let God . . ." Al-Anon can help with
all kinds of control issues. They're the experts. Meetings are friendly
and free.

Affirmations

I can give up my delusions of grandeur.
I am out of control and doing fine.
I'm more than the messes I make.
I'm more than the messes you make.
I can influence, impact, and contribute, but I can't completely con-
trol outcomes.
I can allow things to unfold.

Controlling the Entire Universe?

I am spotless and chaotic, and that's not all I am.
I am older than I was yesterday. I will be even older tomorrow.
I can age gracefully.
I can allow others to have some control, too.
I bonsai trees, not people.
I care about you and don't need to control you.
I support you and don't need to fix you.
I'm not in charge; therefore I am.

13

Change Is Dangerous?

Myth

Change is dangerous and must be avoided.

Truth

Change can feel dangerous, and it can't be avoided.

Inevitably, change happens, ready or not. Sometimes we make it happen. We choose to get married, buy a house, take a vacation, get a dog. Sometimes it just happens. The roof springs a leak, the lover takes a walk, you win the lottery, the tremor becomes an earthquake, the dog has puppies.

One part of us likes life to be tame, stable, and predictable. The other part welcomes change, adventure, challenge, and excitement. Sometimes we get stuck in the middle, scared and ambivalent, unable to move. We want to stay the same and change, take the risk and play it safe, be independent and taken care of, take the new job and keep the one we have, move forward and stand still. The war between these two parts is the war between the settler and the explorer, between Farmer Jones and Indiana Jones.

Like life, change happens when we're making other plans. Without change, we'd be stuck forever celebrating Groundhog Day, sleeping in a crib, toiling at our first job, swooning over our first love, wearing very old clothes. In fact, we're always growing and changing. We keep adding to what we know, what we feel, what we experience. Invisibly and quietly, all the cells in our bodies change every seven years, whether we want them to or not. We can't avoid it.

If we were all Zen masters, we would face change with total equanimity and accept it as natural and inevitable. But most of us resist change. We forget that turning toward the new and unknown only means turning away from the security of the known and familiar.

Fear of the unknown is really not fear but anxiety. Fear happens in the present and dissolves when the threat or danger is past. Anxiety is about fear of the future and can go on forever. Anxiety pumps adrenaline that has nowhere to go, so it turns into stress, acid in the stomach, and a royal pain in the head.

When we're anxious, we anticipate the worst, the what ifs . . .

"What if it doesn't happen?"

"What if it does happen?"

"What if I don't make it?"

"What if I do?"

"What if I'm not perfect?"

"What if . . ."

We're all trying to prepare ourselves for the nine hundred possible scenarios that we just might encounter during the next thirty years. We hire fortune tellers and tarot readers to tell us what's ahead. We cast the I Ching and ask the Ouija Board for answers. We long to be in control of our future. We don't want to be taken by surprise.

Change may be scary, but it's not necessarily dangerous, and mixed feelings are a part of anything new. We may feel some discomfort, some grief about letting go, some sadness about saying good-bye, some pleasure in saying hello, some guilt about feeling excited and moving on. Itching and discomfort may be signs of new growth.

Because growth and change are rarely smooth and consistent, they often require courage and imagination. In any new situation, we have to adjust, experiment, guess, and fake it until we make it. Any change includes moments of regret and a natural urge to retreat. This is always true, whether we're beginning school, graduating, ending a job, entering a relationship, or moving on. We're always taking one step forward, three backward, two to the left, cha cha cha.

In the beginning

Once we didn't believe that change was dangerous. We thought it was fun, exciting, and challenging. The Discovery Channel played in our heads all day long. We were flexible, adjustable, adaptable, and busy gathering new information without judgment or hesitation. We had less clutter in our heads and few negative notions. Everything was new and full of potential.

Left alone, kids are fearless explorers, dogsledding to the South Pole in the back yard, spelunking under the dining room table, flying to Mars for lunch, swinging up into the clouds. "I can do it!" "Don't help me!" "I'll do it myself!" "Let's see what happens if I . . . "

Alas, kids have to be beamed in from the Enterprise for dinner and taught not to play with fire, not to eat the philodendron, and not to cross the street alone. They can't be left entirely on their own to navigate through a world full of real and potential danger.

At best, we all learned what's dangerous and what needs to be avoided, like large and fast-moving objects, especially those that bite. At worst, we were taught to worry about everything that might hurt us. Overly protective parents tried to keep us predictable, safe, and at home. They passed their fears on to us. We were taught to be on guard, to constrict our worlds and make them into safe places where nothing ever goes fast or bites. They worried, and we learned to worry that they were worried. We became timid, shy, and apprehensive about change.

Nevertheless, we all had to learn for better or worse how to cope with change and new beginnings. On the first day of school we found ourselves in an unfamiliar world, not knowing what to expect, who the players were, or where to find the bathroom. We learned important and useful skills that day, like how to stand in line, how to ask questions, and where the blocks were stored. We learned all about how to be a student in that class, in that school. If school was a good experience, with time and practice we became more knowledgeable and confident. We discovered that we could survive the unpredictable, even far from home. This discovery happened again and again as we orbited further and further out into the world.

Some parents feared the worst as they watched us disappear over the horizon. They fretted about us, for us, over us. It was their job. They were agitated and white-knuckled about a world they couldn't control or trust. It was hard for them to let us go to school, drive the car, leave home, grow up, or have sex.

In the present

Since then, most of us have driven a car, left home, grown up, and perhaps even had sex. We survived, probably even had some fun, and we did not fall off the edge of the earth. Despite our family's fears, most of us have moved outside the family's comfort zone, and beyond their horizon. On our journey into adulthood we each carry our unique parcels of inherited fears and expectations.

Change really means moving from the familiar (as in "family") to the strange (as in "stranger"). When we're ready for it, change feels like an opportunity. We feel as powerful and equipped to face the unknown as Indiana Jones in search of the lost ark. Like Indiana, our lives are always in some stage of an adventure cycle. We may be in the first stage, dreaming about an adventure, planning for it by making phone calls, preparing for it by saving money. We may be at the beginning of our adventure (packing or boarding the plane), in the middle of it (standing at the base of the mountain), in the arduous stage (tired and still climbing), near the end of it (seeing the peak and the way down), at the end of it (saying good-byes and returning home). Or, we may be in the final stage, resting from and reflecting on our last adventure (putting the pictures in the album, writing the screenplay), only to begin to dream about the next.

And there are times we just don't want any adventure in our lives. We're feeling safe and comfortable, feet up on the coffee table, snoozing. We may not be ready for the next cycle, but we don't always have the luxury of moving at our own pace. At any time we can be rudely awakened by the knock of change, an uninvited guest at the front door demanding to be let in before we've even put on our socks. We just weren't ready for the earthquake, the rejection on the answering machine, the grim prognosis, or the blue line on the pregnancy test kit. We may feel stunned, off balance, confused, angry, and out of control. Uninvited change can be a real shock to the system.

Uninvited change can also be delightful. The knock on the door might mean winning the lottery, an $80,000 inheritance from Aunt Sophie in Borneo, a loving message on the answering machine, a good prognosis, a blue line on the pregnancy test kit.

Whether they create anguish or delight, unexpected changes can challenge our abilities, tap our deepest resources, and bring us surprising rewards. Even the harshest changes can lead us into unknown territories, opening worlds we never imagined. Forced to make choices we never wanted to make, change can cause us to rethink our most cherished values.

Once upon a time

During a routine checkup, Louise's doctor found a suspicious lump in her breast. He biopsied some tissue and found that it was malignant. Louise's world turned upside down. She had in no way expected this upheaval, and she was not prepared to cope with the deepest issues of living and dying. Suddenly, Louise was forced to make many urgent decisions, and she realized that she had no perfect options. She gathered the best information and support she could. She acknowledged her own limitations and relied on the experience and expertise of others. She struggled with hundreds of what ifs, but she couldn't read the future or anticipate the perfect decision. She could only take one step at a time.

Suddenly, all of Louise's priorities shifted. She had no choice but to face and deal with the changes brought by this uninvited and unwelcome guest. She had to cope. Not simple. Not impossible. She reminded herself that she had struggled with other setbacks before and had somehow muddled through. Others had been in this situation and survived. So could she.

Louise's cancer changed her, and her life. It connected her with a supportive community she'd never imagined. She learned to be more tolerant of her own fragility and the frailty of others. She cherished every day and was continually grateful for the gift of life. She learned not to postpone her dreams, to be generous with love, to meet the world head-on, and not to sweat the small stuff. Although cancer attacked her body, it couldn't defeat her spirit. She did the best she could with the unavoidable changes in her imperfect and unpredictable world.

Sometimes we can hide from change and deny it. Sometimes, like Louise, we can't. We can try to structure our lives to exclude things we don't like and don't want to face. Sometimes that works. We can refuse to fly, never date, never drive, never move, never learn anything, never taste anything new. Sometimes we have the luxury of choosing to change at our own pace. Sometimes we don't.

Once upon a time

Jim hated to ski. Once he had taken a lesson that pushed him to move too fast. Very quickly, he found himself careening downhill, out of control. As his speed increased, so did his panic. His knees locked in fear and he fell again and again. He was in the snow more than he was on the snow, cold, wet, and miserable. After this introductory experience, he decided never to ski again.

Several years later, some friends urged him to spend a weekend on the slopes. They assured him he could stay on the bunny hill and take a lesson. They would all meet at the lodge afterwards. With fear and reluctance, Jim rented gear and signed up for a beginner group lesson. Times had changed. This instructor understood about fear and loss of control. She had all the students put on only one ski. Jim could use his free foot to slow down or stop at any time. He never felt his speed was more than he could handle. He looked strange but felt safe.

Little by little, Jim began to feel some balance and control, first on one side and then on the other. Pretty soon he could move on both skis at once. Sliding through the snow began to feel more comfortable and sometimes even pleasurable. He moved cautiously from the bunny hill to the baby slopes and slowly began to enjoy himself. He began to understand why people might love to ski.

Jim was lucky to have found the right teacher, one who understood fear, panic, and the need for control. She'd helped him find his own pace, his own balance, and a way to make change feel safe.

Change Is Dangerous?

When faced with changes, whenever possible, respect your own timing. When you're afraid, go slow, and get help. If you're still afraid, get a different kind of help. If nothing helps, learn to snowshoe or stay home. Changes are not always required.

Goal

Make friends with change. Allow it to happen. Expect the unexpected. Go with the flow. Accept the inevitable. Don't fight it.

You will get older; people will leave; new people will come; babies will grow; spring will follow winter; some crops will fail; some crops will flourish. The universe has a will and a rhythm of its own. It's best to stay out of its way.

Make change happen. Try a new or different response to an old situation. It changes everything and creates new situations.

Embrace new beginnings. New situations require learning, practice, and the age-old trial and error. Be especially kind to all beginners. Be one.

Stretch yourself

If you are deciding whether or not to make a change, deliberately assess the chances of getting what you want. Pretend you are Lloyd's of London, or Louie the bookie figuring the odds for and against success. Sometimes a risk is a poor one, and sometimes it's a risk worth taking. Anticipate consequences.

Knowing you want to change means you've already begun the process. Trust yourself.

You can slow down the rate of change by tactfully saying,

"Let me think about it. . . . I'll get back to you."

"This is not a good time for me to make big decisions."

"I can't (or won't) decide today. I need to sleep on it."

"I'll think about it tomorrow."

"I have to do this at my own pace."

"I'd like to slow down a little."

When you're ready, take small steps, one ski at a time. Recall the resources you've used in the past. Find folks to go through it with you. Change is easier when you're not alone.

Try this experiment: Let the palms of your hands face each other. Let your fingers interweave in the usual way. Look down and notice which thumb is on top. Now reweave your fingers beginning with the opposite thumb on top. Notice how this feels. Odd? Strange? New? This is the experience of change. If you do it again and again, it will begin to feel more natural and ordinary, just like any new experience.

Practice small changes. Take a new route home from work. Call someone you haven't called in years. Do something you've never done before. Costume yourself in an unusual way. Enjoy the challenge. Let the small change in your pocket be a reminder.

Changing one thing at a time can help you approach your dream of the perfect life. Try this exercise: Close your eyes and imagine a perfect day in your life. Choose an ordinary day, not a special occasion, and visualize every minute of it from the moment you open your eyes in the morning until you go to sleep at night. As you're doing the ordinary things in your life, notice where you are, what you see around you, what you eat, how things smell, what sounds you hear. What color is your perfect toothbrush? Who are your perfect companions? What's your perfect food, dress, work, play, pace, timing? When you open your eyes, write about your perfect day. Read it out loud to yourself or to a friend. How is it different from your life today? What's one thing you can change right now to make your everyday life more like the one you imagined? Hold the long-range vision in sight, but keep the scale small. One change at a time will feed your soul and keep your dream alive.

Recognize one thing in your life that will never change, no matter what you do. You'll always be short or tall or average, male or female. You'll always be from Brooklyn or Des Moines. You probably won't become a prima ballerina or a rocket scientist.

Make your worries about the future useful. Use them to spur you into action. Plan ahead when you can. Do something where you can. If there's nothing you can do, let go, breathe, and pray.

Affirmations

I can change.

I have lots of resources.

I can change my mind.

I can live with my choices.

I am resilient; I can bounce back.

I've handled it before; I'll handle it again.

I'll move when I'm good and ready.

Fear can warn me of danger but not stop me from moving ahead.

I can be scared and change anyway.

I change in order to grow, kicking and screaming all the way.

Life wasn't perfect before this change; it isn't perfect now.

I change; therefore I am.

14

Silence Is Golden?

Myth

If I speak my truth I will hurt other people's feelings.
If I don't say anything, no one will be upset and the
problem will go away. Silence is golden.

Truth

Your truth might or might not hurt anyone's feelings. The problem will
not go away. If silence worked, the problem would already be solved.

Silence speaks loudly. Like body language, it telegraphs powerful
messages without words. Silence can say, "Let's not talk about the
problem. There is no problem. I'm fine. Everything is fine. Let's not
notice the rhinoceros in the living room. (What is that strange jungle
smell?)" When we don't speak, our input, our feelings, our perceptions,
our wisdom, our keen sense of smell remain hidden. The rhino stays
and we disappear.

When we do speak our truth, the other person might have a nervous breakdown, burst into tears, never speak to us again, become
enraged, cut us out of the will. Maybe. Any of those responses tells us a

lot about that person. We learn how they translate our messages into their lives, how much voice they're willing to let us have.

Some people will be relieved when we finally have the confidence to mention that smelly rhino we've all been denying. Others will be shocked at our boldness. It's impossible to list all the potential responses to our verbal daring, but we know the players and we can imagine what they will do and say. When we speak there will certainly be consequences; there are always consequences. We need to assess them, stay calm and firm, breathe.

Every voice is precious. When one voice goes unheard, the story is one-sided and everyone loses. Too often, history is reported only from the victor's point of view, and the voice of the loser is ignored. In a true democracy, all opinions and perceptions are needed to balance the story and complete it. The rich mix of everyone's voice can lead to unexpected possibilities, imaginative solutions, deeper connections, and new truths. Speaking is golden.

In the beginning

It was a child, after all, who shocked the populace into a new knowing by shouting out the truth. The Emperor wasn't wearing any clothes. In fact, he was stark naked. When our parents didn't want to be reminded of the naked truth, they taught us to be silent. They said, "Children should be seen and not heard," or, "If you can't say something nice, say nothing," or something much stronger. So we learned to be quiet and to avoid uttering any unexpected, maybe troublesome, possibly even dangerous, truths.

Picture-perfect families who need to look flawless to themselves and the outside world see speaking the truth as rude, selfish, or unmannerly. But, as Hans Christian Andersen knew, some children can't distinguish between being polite and being honest. If something is talked about in the kitchen, why not in the neighborhood or at school? Little Michael, for instance, was too young to make these fine adult distinctions. One day, for show-and-tell, he proudly announced, "This is Daddy's little pipe, the one he smokes his pot in." Like the Emperor, Daddy was not pleased.

In families where silence equals safety, sorting out when to speak and when to shut up is difficult. When we dare to speak an unacceptable truth, to confuse people with the facts, we might encounter raised eyebrows, eyes rolled to the ceiling in horror and disgust, or any and all of the following retorts:

"You're crazy!"

"That's a lie."

"Shut up and don't ever say that again!"

"Don't be silly."

"You're making no sense."

"You must be overtired."

"I'm really worried about you."

"You're much too sensitive."

"You're a real troublemaker."

"No one else in our family has ever seen a rhino in the living room."

These responses are the bricks in the wall of denial. Rarely will truth, logic, honesty, or hard evidence break through that thick familial wall. If we, as children, were scolded, ridiculed, punished, or beaten for speaking up, we shut up. There was not much we could do except protest, get tired, go underground, and finally join the conspiracy of silence.

Sometimes we were informed our words would damage people we loved. "If you say that, Mommy will get sick, Daddy will have a heart attack, Uncle Joe will have a cow." If we feared that our words could be dangerous or deadly weapons, we put away our powerful words and endured in silence.

We all learned to speak or not to speak the way our families did it. We inherited family rules that had the power of the Ten Commandments, carved in stone. "No ancestor in our family has ever mentioned dreaded beasts like alcoholism, incest, depression, infidelity, sexuality, or rampant rhinos!" To belong, we learned to be like the three monkeys, seeing no evil, hearing no evil, and speaking no evil. In silence, we helped protect the golden image of the perfect family, hoping to get the love and approval we needed to survive.

In the present

If this were a perfect world, speaking our truth would be as sweet as cherry pie. Everyone would understand that our words were only about us, our perceptions, our beliefs, and our feelings. Nobody would ever be hurt by them. We would all hear one another with perfect understanding and appreciation, and all responses would be accepted and honored. We would live forever in verbal bliss on Big Rock Candy Mountain. Alas, this imperfect world is not so sweet and simple. It's a complicated and sticky place where some people will never accept our truths and we will be misinterpreted and judged. When we do speak up, some people won't like what we have to say. Some people may even leave us for a short while or forever. Most people will refuse to hear what they don't want to know.

Although silence may offer us safety for a moment or two, it doesn't really solve anything in the long run. When we don't talk about our problems, they tend to breed and grow. Like untamed rhinos, they may stampede through our living rooms and relationships. Either we speak up about them, or we must pretend that they're not making messes on the rug.

Some rhinos may be pets we brought with us from our childhood homes. Some may be newly hatched young ones. They come in different colors, depending on what we are most afraid to talk about—green like money, purple like passion, grey like illness, striped like prison bars, pink like sexuality, pinstriped like the boss. When we don't speak up, we are usually fearing something, protecting someone, burying something, or denying the rhino within.

As adults, we decide when to stay silent and when and how to speak up for maximum gain and minimal pain. We have three basic choices.

1. We can blow up, scream, snort, and damn the consequences. (Cherry pie will explode onto the ceiling, the walls, and in everyone's faces.)
2. We can shut up, swallow our distress, and get indigestion. (Sometimes, indigestion is the most honorable solution.)
3. We can stand up, speak judiciously, choosing time, place, and tactic carefully. (This works most often in most situations.)

We can act in our own best interests, deciding which rhinos to name, which to discuss, which to throw out the door, which to ignore, which to encourage to sleep on the sofa. Any choice will have consequences. There are always consequences.

Goal

Be brave. Dare to listen to your own words. Cherish your right to be different, to have your own opinions and point of view. Decide when to speak your truth fearlessly. Decide when to be quiet. Reveal yourself wisely. Be sensible. Don't allow yourself to be hit in the face, abandoned, or stomped by rampant rhinos.

Shift your focus. Worry about solving the rhino problem as much as you worry about hurting other people's feelings. Decide what you would like. Do you want the creature dead, tamed, made into a rug, kept in the backyard with the turtles, or thrown out with the trash? Negotiate.

Stretch yourself

Practice speaking your truth in safe places with people you trust. Get chummy with your words. Name any smelly animal in your life. Have a friend or a tape recorder speak your own truth back to you. Repeat it until you feel comfortable. Listen to yourself kindly and well.

Know when to be honest. Honesty is not rudeness or criticism. It's your own truth. Speak about yourself. Use "I" statements without attacking or blaming. Try saying, "This is what I feel and want . . . ," rather than, "This is what's wrong with you. . . . " Your tone of voice matters. More than 90 percent of communication is nonverbal.

Write a letter to someone about a troublesome unspoken truth. Say everything you think and feel on paper. Don't send it. Let it sit in your desk for three weeks. (That's nothing after all these years of silence.) Imagine the reader's response. Choose wisely whether to rewrite it, send it, or trash it. If you choose to send it, let a friend read it first. Be realistic about possible consequences.

As you practice sharing your long-awaited truth, use this handy checklist to control potentially explosive conversations.

1. Start small. Choose a baby rhino to talk about. Don't tackle the biggest bull in the living room first.

2. Timing matters. Don't raise difficult issues when blood sugar is low, when the baby needs a diaper change, in front of anyone's mother, in a crowded elevator, or any time close to April 15.

3. Begin with honest words of kindness and appreciation. Find them.

4. Use "I" sentences that begin with
   "I notice . . ."
   "I wonder . . ."
   "I feel . . ."
   "I believe . . ."
   "I smell . . ."

5. Avoid TNT language, such as
   "You should / ought . . ."
   "You always / never . . ."

6. Avoid name calling, threats, blaming, ridicule, nagging, or sarcasm. Don't use a baseball bat to shoo a fly.

7. Make requests instead of demands or ultimatums. Say, "I would like . . . ," instead of, "You must . . . ," or, "You have to . . . or else . . ."

8. Listen kindly and well to others' responses. Validate their truth. They also need to be heard.

9. Aim for getting what you both need. When both of you win, no one loses except the rhino.

10. Listen to how other people speak hard truths. Imitate what works. You're learning a new skill here; it's wise to apprentice yourself.

11. Invest in a good book on communication skills. Practice and rehearse with friends. Fake it until you make it.

12. Congratulate yourself every time you risk naming the rhino and staying clear about what you want. Enjoy your own boldness and imagination.

13. If all else fails, don't be afraid to call the experts. Some rhinos are just too big and ornery to handle alone.

Affirmations

I can speak up for maximum gain and minimum pain.
My truth is golden.
My truth is only mine.
I can allow myself to be seen and heard.
I can choose when to speak and when to stay silent.
My words won't kill anyone, and no one's words will kill me.
I can learn to speak so others will hear me.
I can listen to other people's truths.
I can handle the consequences of speaking my truth.
I can have a rhino for a pet no matter what anyone says.
I speak; therefore I am.

15

Happiness Is Hazardous?

Myth

Happiness is hazardous. Pleasure is perilous. Ecstasy is unthinkable.
If I let myself be too happy, disaster will follow.

Truth

Disaster doesn't naturally follow happiness—neither does pain, shame, or guilt, unless you invite them along for the ride. Happiness is not necessarily hazardous. Pleasure is not inevitably perilous. Ecstasy is thinkable.

Happiness is just a temporary state of bliss that you don't deserve. You don't deserve anguish, either. Neither happiness nor pain is about deserving or being good enough. In fact, the root of the word *happiness* means good luck or chance. Happiness just happens, and you can survive it. You might even learn to enjoy it.

Remember what Mom never said: "All *bad* things come to an end." Good things, too. If you let yourself be happy, something else will follow. If you let yourself be miserable, something else will follow. Happiness ends. So does misery. Nothing is permanent. You can choose whether to live your life as Winnie the Pooh, the hopeful, optimistic bear, or Eeyore, the gloomy, pessimistic donkey.

In the beginning

As babies, we were probably happy as long as we were warm, dry, fed, and loved. Those basics don't change much over the years. We change.

Some families encourage happiness and good times. Such encouragement is a lifelong gift to children, who learn to accept, expect, and welcome the joy in their own lives.

Some families don't celebrate. They don't make room for exuberance, enthusiasm, or joy. For them, happiness is no laughing matter. They rain on their children's parades and have no parades of their own. These serious families fret. They see happiness as a frivolous distraction from the primary and necessary business of worrying. They want their children to worry with them. If the kids aren't worried, the parents have to do it for them. They see danger everywhere and keep their children ever vigilant and on edge. There's no way for children to be happy when they continually hear warnings like these:

"Be careful."

"Look out!"

"Slow down."

"Think and plan ahead."

"Don't forget."

"Look before you leap."

"Watch out! You might get hurt."

Some families clip their children's natural exuberance, joy, and excitement: "Children should be seen and not heard."

"Settle down! Calm down! Quit acting like a baby!"

"Don't make a silly face or your face will freeze like that."

"Don't laugh so loud. You'll wake Daddy."

"Parties are a waste of time and money."

"It always rains on picnics and parades."

Envious families hate anyone else's happiness or good fortune. They believe it's downright sinful for the children or the folks down the street to look or feel better than they do. They're party poopers, wet blankets, scornful and bitter, ready to pounce on the first hint of success. They live as though good things and good feelings are scarce. They believe that there's just not enough happiness to go around. Their attitudes and behavior are based on notions of scarcity:

"There's no room at the top."

"If I can't march in this parade, no one can."

"If you're happy, I can't be. If I'm happy, you can't be."

"Only one of us gets to be happy at a time. No sharing."

Some families believe that everything and everyone can and should be scrutinized, evaluated, and improved. No one ever passes inspection. Membership in these families comes from participating in nit-picking and flaw-finding hunts. After all, there's always room for improvement.

The most rigid families value discipline over joy, rules over flexibility or creativity. They believe that happy children are a sign of lazy parenting, that praise and compliments are unnecessary. Pats on the head only make children egotistical, prideful, self-indulgent, and spoiled rotten. Their motto is "spare the rod and spoil the child." They punish with no warning—tenderly stroke a child's cheek, then smack it. No wonder happiness seems dangerous.

Many of us found our greatest childhood pleasures outside our homes, inside books, inside our imaginations, with our friends, at the neighbor's, at grandma's. Some of us were applauded at school for scoring at soccer, winning the spelling bee, playing the tuba, clowning around, being really good at hopscotch. Some of us took refuge at the park, at the library, in a tree house, at the Y, at the vacant lot, on the street. We might have learned, in these situations, that happiness without hazard was possible, that we could be gleeful without having to pay for it.

Happiness can also seem dangerous if feeling good got paired up with an unexpected shock. Picture a child, proud and exuberant, riding her new bike. Suddenly she is frightened by a car backfiring and makes a quick movement that destroys her balance. She falls off the bike, badly injuring her knee. Bingo. Happiness and danger get paired, stick together, and glue themselves deeply in our consciousness, warning us that too much exuberance and pleasure can be hazardous to our health.

In the present

Confusion rains on all of us. Our biology insists that we turn toward pleasure and away from pain. But our experience can teach us to be wary of pleasure, hide from happiness, discount delight, and shrink from success. We don't take time to savor the chocolate when we're worried about the calories. We don't enjoy the children when we're worried about their manners. We don't celebrate our successes when we doubt our own worth. Our negativity can nibble at our capacity for pleasure and keep us anxious, cautious, and judgmental.

Many thinkers and writers have had a lot to say about the serious business of being happy. They, too, radiate contradiction.

> "One half of the world cannot understand the pleasures of the other."
> —Jane Austen, *Emma*

> "A lifetime of happiness! It would be hell on earth."
> —George Bernard Shaw, *Man and Superman*

> "There's no duty we so much underrate as the duty of being happy."
> —Robert Louis Stevenson, *Virginibus Puerisque*

We are experts at creating our own unhappiness. We invent catastrophes, foresee frightening futures, invent a thousand tortures to punish ourselves for feeling good. Our negative fantasies keep us subdued and contained. This is the upside-down Disneyland in our heads. And the rides never stop. As others have already noticed, being happy depends on our perceptions, not our circumstances.

> "We are never so happy nor so unhappy as we imagine."
> —Francois de la Rochefoucauld, *Maximes*

> "Happiness generally depends more on the Opinion we have of Things, than on the Things themselves."
> —Thomas Fuller, *Gnomologia*

> "All happiness is in the mind."
> —H. G. Bohn, *Handbook of Proverbs*

Happiness Is Hazardous?

> "Happiness is an imaginary condition, formerly often attributed by the living to the dead, now usually attributed by adults to children, and by children to adults."
>
> —Thomas Szasz, *The Second Sin*

We're so afraid of being happy that when good fortune arrives, we cover our mouths, lower our voices, and knock on wood. These superstitious responses are ancient devices once believed to protect folks from evil creatures who might envy and steal their good fortune. Knocking on wood may be a very old custom to call forth the benign spirits of trees, to ward off any lurking or jealous spirit. Fearful of happiness, we deny our good fortune and underplay it by being afraid that lightning will strike and disaster will follow.

We scare ourselves that any success will backfire. Any achievement might call attention to our imperfections. We might be discovered for the frauds we believe we really are. To be visible is to be a target, a sitting duck, attracting attention and inviting criticism. We fear that the world will sit around in cafes, drinking cafe latte and discussing the flaws that we've worked so hard, and so unsuccessfully, to hide.

We try to talk ourselves out of happiness, to give it away: "I've been so bad, I've done so many terrible things, I don't deserve to be happy. The universe must have made a mistake. My good fortune surely belongs to someone better than I am." In truth, someone will always be better than we are. Someone will always be worse. The universe doesn't care. The universe shares. Sometimes everyone gets to have some joy, whether they deserve it or not.

Some of us can't let ourselves be happy if others are suffering. "If I'm happy, I'm being insensitive to the plight of those less fortunate. It's unseemly and downright selfish to be joyful when there's pain in the world." In truth, even when we suffer terribly the rest of the world is no better off. Actually, when we're happy and feeling abundant, we tend to be kinder and more generous to others. Our positive energy lights up our little corner of the universe. When we're unhappy, we tend to be more self-absorbed and live in a world of mirrors. We see only our own negative images and have no energy for others. When we feel bad we spread darkness, and no one, except our worst enemy, feels better.

Happiness doesn't last. It will end, and when it ends, we may feel let down, a little sad, nostalgic—but we don't die. The best we can do is live fully in the moments of joy, savoring them and then letting them go.

> "Happiness is probably only a passing accident. For a moment or two, the organism is irritated so little that it is not conscious of it; for the duration of that moment, it is happy."
> —H. L. Mencken, *American Mercury*, March 1930

Goal

Be courageous. Challenge negativity. Challenge anyone who tries to rain on your parade. Challenge your own superstitions. Defy the dark fears that dampen your joy.

Take charge of your own happiness. Expect it. Let it happen. Allow yourself to feel it. Let it show. It looks good on you. Share it. The world needs all the good feelings it can get.

> "Be happy. It's one way of being wise."   —Colette

> "The most evident token and apparent sign of true wisdom is a constant and unconstrained rejoicing."   —Montaigne

Expand your definition of happiness to include some other voices, like those below:

> "Happiness is a delicate balance between what one is and what one has."   —J. H. Denison

> "A happy life must be, to a great extent, a quiet life, for it is only in an atmosphere of quiet that true joy can live."
> —Bertrand Russell, *The Conquest of Happiness*

> "Happiness? That's nothing more than health and a poor memory."   —Albert Schweitzer

> "Happiness is having a large, loving, close-knit family in another city."   —George Burns

> "Happiness, to some, elation
> Is to others, mere stagnation."   —Amy Lowell, *Happiness*

124

Happiness Is Hazardous?

"[Happiness is] no creditor at the door and nobody sick."
—William Scarborough, *Chinese Proverbs*

"Happiness is a warm puppy."   —Charles Schulz, 1963

"It is neither wealth nor splendor, but tranquility and occupation, which give happiness."
—Thomas Jefferson, *Letter to Mrs. A. S. Marks*

"Happiness? It is an illusion to think that more comfort means more happiness. Happiness comes of the capacity to feel deeply, to enjoy simply, to think freely, to risk life, to be needed."   —Storm Jameson, *Reader's Digest*, January 1948

"If you would be happy for a day, buy a bottle of wine. If you would be happy for a week, kill a pig. If you would be happy for a month, get married. If you would be happy for the rest of your life, be a gardener."   —Old Chinese proverb

Stretch yourself

"Happiness is a habit—cultivate it."
—Elbert Hubbard, *Epigrams*

Make others happy. Acknowledge the good stuff. Smile and appreciate competence, kindness, good temper, generous acts. Be generous. Send compliments to the chef, the bus driver, the mailman, the street cleaner.

Make yourself happy. Acknowledge your good stuff, first quietly, then investigate bragging, boasting, celebrating. Gradually experiment with loud and blissful exuberance and the occasional ticker tape parade.

Take ten minutes daily to notice and appreciate the tiniest sweet stuff of the last twenty-four hours. Tolerate the initial discomfort of pure enjoyment, the shock to your negative belief system. At the risk of sounding very peculiar, tell someone. Failing that, write it down. We tend to keep journals when we're distressed; try keeping one to record and acknowledge all the good stuff.

When happiness seems far out of reach, conjure moments of pure delight when you were four, eight, or twelve. Remember the favorite toy you dragged everywhere, building forts under the kitchen table, playing checkers with your grandfather, diving off the high board, getting a new puppy. Notice how your grownup endorphins snap, crackle, and pop as your body remembers childhood pleasures.

Get simple. Find simple pleasures. The big complicated pleasures come and go, but the small ones are as close as a cool drink of water on a hot summer day.

> "The world is so full of a number of things,
> I'm sure we should all be as happy as kings."
> —Robert Louis Stevenson, *A Child's Garden of Verses*

> "Don't worry. Be happy." —Bobby McFerrin

Affirmations

I can make room for optimism.

I choose whether my glass is half full or half empty.

I choose whether to be Eeyore or Pooh.

I'm in charge of my negativity.

My happiness depends on me, not on anyone else.

My happiness won't last; neither will my misery. I can enjoy them both.

I can be happy right now.

I can eat dessert first.

I have been really lucky in my life.

I will let happiness continue to find me.

I can be imperfect and happy.

I'm happy; therefore I am.

16

I Am What I Achieve?

Myth

I must be productive, work hard, achieve. I am what I accomplish.

Truth

You are far more than you will ever accomplish. You are a human being, not just a human doing. If work is the value you live by, you may be slaving for a boss like Simon Legree. Are you the overseer who cracks the whip and never lets you rest? Are you a slave to your work, your projects, or your productions? You may be a closet workaholic. Take a moment of well-earned personal time and see if you fit the perfect overworker profile.

The Workaholic Pop Quiz
Instruction: Check all responses that apply.
__ You are constantly busy.
__ The idea of delegating any responsibility strikes you as totally ridiculous.
__ You typically work overtime, doing more than is humanly possible.

__ You leap tall stacks of paper in a single bound.

__ Your life and everyone in it take second place to your productivity.

__ Your neck and shoulders are always tight. Your chiropractor is buying a yacht.

__ You believe no one can ever do the job as well as you can.

__ You never believe the job was done well enough.

__ You are exhilarated by exhaustion.

__ You function frazzled and fried to a crisp.

__ You are scheduled so tightly that there is no time for anything to go wrong. No flat tires, no allergies allowed.

__ "Relaxation" is a dirty word.

If you have checked several of these responses, you have bought into the American Dream, the do-aholic Type-A nightmare.

The American Dream insists that to be perfect we must toil harder, think bigger, strive longer, and make more money. This dream is one of those terrible tossing and turning nightmares that can go on for thirty years. It's about struggling and striving and falling short. It's about never being satisfied, never having or being enough, never feeling finished, always feeling inadequate.

The modern Simon Legree says, "You could, should, would make it to the top, if only you put in a few more hours every day, a few more days every month, a few more months every year." Simon never mentions that this intense striving causes burnout, acid indigestion, headaches, stress-related illness, and very tired, grumpy people longing for rest. There's nothing wrong with wanting to do our best job. The trouble begins when nothing we do seems good enough.

Other cultures thrive without the Puritan ethic we inherited from the folks on the Mayflower. In some very civilized places, people have leisurely afternoon meals, then take naps, work late afternoons, listen to music, dance, and spend time with their children. Some very civilized people meditate, move slowly, refuse to be stressed out, feel satisfied and content. And the necessary work still gets done.

But we hotshot, fast-lane, high-rolling, consummate achievers often forget that even the fastest racing car needs pit stops to cool down and refuel. Even if we are Ferraris or Porsches, we need to know when we're over-revving, when we're close to overheating, when we're shifting into cruise control, when we're skidding out of control, when we're slowing to a stop. Even our excellent brains, so beautifully designed for speed and accuracy, need to shift gears. They can only run effectively for ninety-minute cycles without a rest. When we drive ourselves at breakneck speed, we're usually exceeding our natural human speed limit. Check the machinery. The pace that works best for your year and model may be different from the one at which you're driving. Consider what speed is really right for your age and condition.

Work goes on with us or without us. We are not indispensable. One day, at retirement or by changes in circumstance, our work life will end. Breathe. Inhale. Exhale. Life will go on.

In the beginning

Three-year-olds squeal, "I can do it! I can spread the peanut butter on the cracker! I can push the stroller! I can hold the baby and not drop him!" Children (and adults) take great pride in doing things well, show great joy when they master new skills. Some parents are delighted with their children's newfound competence. Others feel nervous or frightened by it. Most feel both.

Some parents want perfection without mistakes, results without experimentation: no peanut butter on the table cloth, no spilled juice, no broken crayons, no skinned knees, no muddy shoes. They ask, "Why weren't you more careful?" "Why didn't you try harder?" "Why didn't you get it right the first time?" "Why did you miss that one math problem?" "Why didn't you make that soccer goal?" "You need to do things better, faster, smarter, sooner, neater, harder." No accomplishment is ever good enough for parents who want perfect children.

Kids easily catch the virus of perfectionism from parents who are already infected.

Once upon a time

Sheila's mother was not just a doer, but a carrier of the Super-doer Virus. She saw herself as indispensable. She raised extremely tidy and well-behaved children. She met all the requirements of a demanding job and kept the house immaculately clean. She grew prize-winning roses, cooked meals that included three nourishing items on a plate, and kept the wheels of the family perfectly oiled. She was endlessly busy and always exhausted.

Sheila's father was not a Super-doer. He was a laid-back, easygoing kind of guy, not infected with perfectionism. He worked a lot, but he never struggled as much as his wife did. He didn't get stressed, frazzled, or fried. He was relatively content, thoroughly fun-loving, and relaxed. Shiela's mother was furious with him for enjoying himself when she was stressed out twenty-six hours a day.

Sheila grew up to see life from her mother's perspective. Like Mother, she disdained her father's way of being in the world. She was afraid of being one of the bad guys—lazy, slow, playful, loose, happy, not living up to her potential—like Dad. Like Mother, Sheila denied the fun-loving, easygoing, relaxed part of herself. She was convinced that Mom's way was the only correct way to be a success in the world. Thus, the Super-doer Virus gets passed on from one do-aholic generation to the next.

All families pass on strong feelings, values, and messages about work. Some Super-doer families disdain anyone lying under a tree reading a book or just staring at the moon. They condemn others for being lazy, slow, or remarkably unproductive. If playfulness, daydreaming, relaxing, and sleeping late were demeaned as slovenly and dangerous, you may have decided early on never to be caught napping.

We don't necessarily catch this Super-doer Virus directly from our families. Workaholism is in the air everywhere. We inhale it from phrases like these:

"Busy hands are happy hands; idle hands are the devil's workshop."

"No pain, no gain."

"Work before play."

"Work is its own reward."

"Keep busy or you'll never amount to anything."

"Work cures all ills."

"If you have some time to kill, work it to death."

We were all asked before sixth grade, "What are you going to be when you grow up?" We were all told to work harder, longer, better to live up to our potential. These messages kept us vulnerable to any Super-doer Virus that came along. No one was dispensing antiviral messages.

"Take your time."

"Find the rhythm that's right for you."

"Let yourself be a kid."

"Relax, you've got your whole life to work hard."

"Learn at your own pace."

"There's no hurry."

"Don't rush. We'll wait for you."

How different our lives would have been if we'd grown up in a virus-free world.

In the present

As grownups, we get to check our own vital signs to see if we carry the Super-doer Virus, the plague of industrialized society. This virus is especially lethal for women who enter the workplace and don't (or can't) give up the seventy thousand demands of being a homemaker. Too often, women believe they have to do it all perfectly—the job, the house, the kids, the world. Being merely mortal, they feel guilty, as if they're shirking responsibility, when they can't handle it all. This is a critical problem in single-parent families. Many super women are engaged in life or death struggles with the Super-doer Virus.

Some of us, juggling jobs, family, and other obligations, need to be very busy for some years. Some of us truly enjoy our busyness. Some of us stay busy when we don't need or want to, out of fear or habit. Some of us never learned to rest without seeing ourselves as lazy. Some of us find the idea of resting positively terrifying, thinking, "Down time is dead time," or "If I stop, I'll die." Some of us expect to feel lost and unstructured and tell ourselves, "I'll be bored," "What is there to think about?" "What will I do with myself?" and "How will I fill all that time?" These beliefs make it hard to take a long hot bath, relax in the sun for half an hour, read a totally engrossing trashy novel, or take a nap without feeling uneasy, selfish, and irresponsible.

Work can be great. At its best, work offers some very large external rewards, including status, a community of colleagues, self-definition, structure, and money. It can give us the satisfaction of completing a task, meeting a challenge, and the pleasure of our own competence. At its best, work also offers large internal rewards. It can help us realize we are creative, valuable, smart, capable, and accomplished. Sometimes, work can be a blessing.

Work can also be a curse. Paradoxically, even when our jobs or careers are most rewarding, we can feel trapped by their endless challenges and demands. When we can't slow down, it's easy to get addicted to the doing, the performing, the climbing up, up, up those career ladders. Work can become our identity, our family, our name, our purpose in life, and the only measure of our success. It can run our lives if we let it.

Despite many changes in the workplace, the culture still defines good guys as hard-working, serious, punctual, responsible, capable, neat, and rich. (Remember that Sheila's father was the bad guy.) Most adult Super-doers want to be good guys, just like we wanted to be good kids, acknowledged and applauded by our parents. Now we hope our bosses and supervisors will give us the appreciation and love we wanted from our parents.

Bosses and parents have much in common. They are in charge. They make the rules. They evaluate us and our performance. They have bigger chairs and desks, bigger windows, and more phones than we do. Being a worker can be a lot like being a kid—smaller office, smaller chairs and desks, no windows—with lots of leftover kid feelings. The boss's simple statement, "I want to see you in my office; we need to talk," can set off a fire alarm inside our heads. Like an eight-year-old, we can obsess about eighty-six things we've done wrong and be sure the boss is going to get on our case about eighty-two of them. We can hear our mothers saying, "I know what you've done. Just wait till your father gets home."

When we see our bosses as parents, we give them too much power. It's not good for us and it's not good for them. When our bosses are our only source of approval, just as our parents once were, our self-worth can be tied to their assessment of us. When our performance doesn't earn pats on the head and bigger allowances, we can feel worthless and frustrated. So we become do-aholics, passionately striving to get everything we missed when we were eight.

This is a fruitless and thankless endeavor and really confuses the issue. It's just too late. We're not eight anymore. Whether we always believe it or not, we're adults, and our real worth doesn't depend on our bosses' evaluations. In truth, we will always be imperfect employees, just as we were imperfect children, and our bosses will never be the perfect parents we never had.

Once upon a time

Perfectly competent Carl was a community health worker. He had a sparkling resume. His bosses and colleagues all recognized his competence, his skill, and his contributions to the field. He was asked to organize and promote a statewide conference for health providers. It was a huge responsibility, and Carl was flattered that he was invited to be in charge. He happily agreed to take on the monumental task.

Carl managed to do it all, working eighteen hours a day for weeks, and going into the office on weekends. He never rested. He hardly slept. He quit karate. He stopped walking the dog, seeing friends, and playing racquetball. He was completely dedicated and focused, determined to create a perfect conference. He handled a thousand details and fielded a million phone calls. The conference was a huge success. Participants filled out glowing evaluations and offered appreciative feedback.

Soon after the conference was over, Carl fell into an unexpected depression. Everyone thought it had gone perfectly, but he knew it hadn't. There had been many small glitches, but he found himself obsessing over one ornery microphone in one seminar room. No one had been able to stop it from squealing, and the presenter had trouble being heard over the interference. Carl couldn't let himself forget it. He told himself, "I should have double-checked all the equipment. I should have been more careful. I should have done more." He began to question every mistake, his own worth, and the worth of the whole project. "If this one thing went wrong, other things were probably screwed up, too. The whole conference was really a mess. People say it was fine, but they're just being nice, trying not to hurt my feelings." This is the Super-doer Virus at fever pitch.

Carl tormented himself, feeling angry, inadequate, unworthy, and a failure. Finally, he talked with his friendly neighborhood therapist about how crazed he felt. Even though the conference was clearly a success, he had set himself up for failure. Lurking behind all his vigilance and superproductivity were his secret ambitions. He wanted to be perfectly productive, flawless, tireless, even saintly. He wanted to save the world. He couldn't. He wanted to be Superman. He wasn't.

Carl lived in a universe full of unreliable electronics, like microphones that didn't work perfectly. Every glitch in any system reminded him of his own glitches. He was inadequate. The world was not letting him save it. He was not approaching sainthood. Even the most successful conference couldn't change Carl's limited view of himself. Even when he was superhuman, he, the conference, and the world were still less than perfect. How unfair!

Carl needed to be reminded that he was more than his awesome productivity. He was both flawed and good enough. Sometimes, he was even better than good enough. And he wasn't Father Martin Luther Kennedy Damien. Occasionally he got to feel like Superman, but he was really Clark Kent.

Like Carl, we can and often do avoid noticing our imperfections by overcompensating and becoming attached to busyness. Our hyperactivity and superproductivity can help us avoid intimacy (Who has time?), companionship (That doesn't matter anyway.), and real life (That's too terrifying.). Instead, we get addicted to the adrenaline rush of competition and success. We seek more and more power, status, money, things, and we begin to believe that those who have the most toys win. We feel driven to jump onto the next bandwagon, meet the next challenge. Climbing to the top may be a part of human nature, but no one has ever seen a tombstone with the inscription "I wish I had worked more. I wish I had played less."

In the race to accomplish, we can lose our imperfect selves in our own dust. And when the dust settles, there we are—imperfect, human, and dusty. We forget that we have other options, like slowing down, stopping for a while, finding nourishment in other ways. We could get out the picnic basket, put down the blanket, enjoy the view, and rest. We could lie down and watch the clouds go by. We could ask ourselves some important questions: Who am I competing with, really? Who are the role models for my frantic behavior? Whose life am I living anyway? What am I running from? What could I let go of? Who will I leave behind? At this point in my life, what's the right rhythm, the right balance between work and everything else? How can I get there from here?

I Am What I Achieve?

Believe it or not, we can choose not to abuse ourselves with work. We can choose how we want to spend our time. We can decide how work fits into our lives and how busy we really need to be.

Goal

If this is a time in your life when you need to focus on work, find a way to love it or at least to make it work for you.

Shift your attention from the perfect product to steady progress. Progress means taking one step at a time. Break big tasks into small steps. This keeps you from feeling overwhelmed. And you will get somewhere. Mother Teresa didn't set out to save the world, just to help a few folks in need.

Balance your workload.

Stop giving 110 percent everywhere; choose where to put your energy.

Set some limits.

Make a commitment to manage yourself.

Schedule periods of downtime—time to spend with family, friends, in the natural world, with art and music, alone with your mind and body.

Spend time doing what you love to do. You don't have to explain.

Notice that there is a whole other world out there, a Shangri-la beyond the Himalayas of work.

Turn intensive hanging out into an art form.

Remember, you are a human being as well as a human doing.

Stretch yourself

No homework. Take time to rest and play.

Affirmations

I choose when to take my time and when to hurry.

Being unhurried is good for me and an excellent model for everyone around me.

I take time to play without having to suffer for it.

Pit stops allow me to go farther and longer.

I can balance work and play.

I am determined not to overwork and stress myself into a heart attack.

I am more than any task I do or anything I accomplish.

I'm withdrawing my candidacy for sainthood.

I work and play; therefore I am.

17

Never Too Rich or Too Thin?

Myth

I can never be too rich or too thin.

Truth

Yes you can, and you can die trying. We can kill ourselves working too hard to get rich. We can kill ourselves eating too little to get thin. We can feel so bad about ourselves, our bodies, and our bank accounts that we're even willing to risk our lives to increase our holdings, to reduce our size.

Billions of dollars are spent annually to convince us that we have too little money and too many pounds. Our dissatisfactions fuel the weight-loss and financial-planning industries. The pros who know how to push all our buttons pressure us into feeling unhappy, needy, inadequate, and dissatisfied with ourselves. They keep us trying and buying. Notice how few dollars are spent to build our self-esteem, encourage us to care for our health, value our imaginations, support our creativity, or feed our spirits. No wonder we're never okay with how we look or what we have.

We try to manage our inner distress by fixing our outsides. Seasonally we repackage ourselves. We shrink-wrap our suffering bodies and surround ourselves with more stuff, in the hope that our innards will feel better when our outtards are perfect.

Now consider the opposite. If we dared to feel adequate and satisfied, we could probably undermine America's entire economic infrastructure. If we felt secure and happy enough to consume less, we could cause the market to collapse and the value of the dollar to drop like a stone. As good citizens concerned for the welfare of the nation, it is our patriotic duty to believe we're too fat and too poor, and to kill ourselves trying to trim the scales and fatten our wallets, shrink our shirt sizes and expand our portfolios.

Why aren't the richest and thinnest people totally relaxed, serene, cheerful, good-tempered, and completely satisfied with their lives? Did Jackie O. seem happy? Did Ari O.? What about Rockefeller? Howard Hughes? Michael Jackson? Karen Carpenter?

Maybe happiness isn't about being rich or thin. Maybe we already have everything we need—perhaps more than everything. Maybe the Wizard of Oz was right—we're already home, we already have the heart, the brains, and the courage that we thought we could find somewhere else. Maybe we're already rich enough, thin enough, perfect enough just the way we are. Maybe we're already swimming in grace.

In lots of countries, being fat or poor is not a sin. In America, we tend to worship money (more for men) and looks (more for women). Men (mostly) earn status, power, and control by being rich, being a somebody. Women (mostly) earn power and control by being young and beautiful, having a great body, and feeling like a nobody unless they have a Mr. Somebody. More than men, women are defined by their packaging. They're supposed to be forever young and svelte, like Barbie. Men are supposed to be wealthy and accomplished, like Ken.

The culture encourages this. Sean Connery changes, becomes grizzled, older, wider, and wiser. His leading ladies are always typecast ingenues, forever thin, flawless, twenty-two. They're traded in for a new model every few years. Male newscasters get older and more distinguished; aging anchorwomen are replaced. Female talk show hosts worry about their weight; male talk show hosts worry about their politics. Women lawyers are judged by the power of their clothes; men lawyers are judged by the power of their arguments. Women are told so often that their accomplishments don't really matter that they begin to discount their own skills. The whole culture loses out when smart, competent women spend prime time worrying what color eye shadow will match their shoes.

Imagine if the messages for men and women got mixed up in that big mailbag in the sky and the myths were gender-shifted. Consider how our world would be different if the power of women was in money and men's power was in being slender, attractive, glamorous, and sweetly generous. It would follow that women can never be too rich and men can never be too thin. In this scenario, women are out in the competitive dog-eat-dog world of business and finance. Men look attractive on women's arms. They're decorative. They do the caretaking and nurturing. Society insists that these activities are proper for men. Their emotional fulfillment comes from giving to others and putting others' needs before their own.

Men are in charge of traditional family values. Women are in charge of earning and spending the money. Men are responsible for homemaking, keeping the house tidy, and being sensitive to women's special needs. Good men monitor their wives' cholesterol, alcohol consumption, and general health. They remember and celebrate all birthdays and anniversaries. Men color coordinate kitchens. Women negotiate real estate contracts. Men get their hair and nails done at the handsome parlor. They worry about their weight. Father's Day gifts are pressure cookers, vacuum cleaners, flowers, chocolate, and perfume. Mother's Day gifts are laptop computers, prestige pens, hunting rifles, power saws, and hammocks.

Men aspire to be secretaries, dental hygienists, nurses, teachers, waiters. They're the power behind the throne, the cheerful souls who raise the children and keep the queendom running. They seem less attractive as they get older, and their wives often replace them with younger, more vigorous, less intelligent or demanding men. In order to remain desirable and pleasing, men are expected to work out at the gym, diet, and always be attractively groomed, especially when the hard-working wife comes home from a tough day at the office.

Women are seen as more valuable the older they get. Greying hair and a few laugh lines around the eyes make them seem more distinguished, sexier, more valuable, wiser. Elder stateswomen, judges, professors, doctors, intelligent newscasters, and aging actresses are the most desirable women.

When a marriage ends, it's usually the man's fault. He was probably not understanding enough about his wife's passion for work and her deep friendships with other men or women. He probably didn't meet his wife's needs and was probably too needy and demanding himself. Unreasonably, he expected her to make his life meaningful. He was often sexually unresponsive, insensitive, and unimaginative. He did not understand the fragility of the female ego. He didn't monitor his sexual rhythms to accommodate hers. He took her suggestions as personal criticism. No wonder the marriage failed.

Confused and wearied by complex roles and endless demands, men often escape into romance novels. Feeling insecure, they read lots of self-help books to better understand their mates. They read *Men Who Love Too Much* and its troubling sequel, *Women Who Love Too Little*. They often seek counseling. Most men feel inadequate, worry, eat to soothe their anxieties, and consider antidepressants. No wonder there's a 51 percent divorce rate.

A society that explained gender differences in a different way might assume that without predictable hormonal cycles, men could erupt at any time, making them irrational, unpredictable, and potentially disastrous in the workplace. Men's obsession with sex makes them unreliable managers. Men's aggressiveness makes them unable to negotiate reasonable international policies. Their innate competitiveness makes them less cooperative than women. They cause friction and dissension wherever they work. Women's predictable cycles enable them to plan ahead and adapt to hormonal changes. Their negotiating experience enables them to drive hard bargains without giving offense.

Meanwhile, back in the real world, each gender is still struggling with its own demands and its own illusions. Even though things are changing as the world turns, thin and relationships continue to be women's issues, and rich and worldly are still about men.

In the beginning (Rich)

Most immigrants came to America seeking asylum, opportunities, and a better life. They were hungry for food, freedom, and control over their own destiny. It was said that in America everything was possible. This was the land of milk and honey, where you could escape the old class system and become wealthy, even if you started as one of the unwashed. The streets were paved with gold. The sky was the limit. Anyone could go from rags to riches. Any boy born in a log cabin could be president. Any girl who was pretty enough could marry a rich man and live a life of leisure. Anyone could have it all.

The underbelly of this message was that if men didn't strike it rich, there was something wrong with them. They didn't have enough grit, imagination, brains, stick-to-itiveness, or persistence. Even now, many people believe, deep down, that men who don't make it are somehow lazy or defective. Women who don't make it in the relationship market are still seen as unfulfilled old maids, dried-up spinsters who are robbing their parents of grandchildren.

The sad truth is that the American dream has never been equally available to everyone. It is a great dream, but limited, truer, and much easier for some people than for others. We all grew up believing it, but one day we woke up to a real life much more complicated than any dream. Wealth is not inevitable; hard work or good looks don't guarantee riches or marriage. Some make it and some don't. It isn't fair.

The American dream of prosperity is different for everybody. It varies according to each family's history and beliefs about earning and spending. Children raised during the Great Depression of the thirties have different attitudes than children of post–World War II affluence. Some families never had any money. Some had too much. Some lived within their incomes. Some borrowed. Some blew it. Some went into debt and couldn't get out. Some stole for necessity or for pleasure.

Some families had to choose between having breakfast or having supper, paying the rent or putting gas in the car. Some could afford a new car every year, investments in land, art, vacations, education, stocks and bonds. Some families invested in gambling, booze, cigarettes, and hot times.

Every family has its own rules for spending and saving. Some value saving. Remember going to the bank and opening your first savings account, having your very own bankbook? Some love to spend. Remember taking your dollar to the store and having infinite choices? You can learn a lot about how you "do" money now by remembering how your family did it then.

Here are a few favorite family financial fables. Find yours.

1. We never talk about money.
2. Money is all we talk about.
3. Life is uncertain. Save your money for a rainy day.
4. Life is short. Spend today. Worry tomorrow.
5. Debt is shameful. Never borrow. Only buy what you can afford.
6. Debt is necessary and smart. Always use the bank's money.
7. Never buy retail.
8. You get what you pay for. Buy the best.
9. Always budget.
10. Forget budgets. Be spontaneous. You can always rob Peter to pay Paul.
11. We're poor no matter how much we have.
12. We're rich no matter how little we have.
13. Only men really understand money.
14. Only women spend too much money.
15. My children should have more than I ever had.
16. My children can take care of themselves. I'm spending all I make.
17. Money is the root of all evil.
18. Money makes the world go 'round.
19. Work hard. Do a day's work for a day's pay.
20. Make money while you sleep.
21. Spend it. There are no debtors' prisons.
22. Save it. The wolves are howling at the door.
23. There's a perfect way to do money.
24. There's no perfect way to do money.

In the present (Rich)

In relationships, money can be dynamite. It's the number one land mine that explodes in most living rooms. The fuses are the disagreements over who has it, who needs it, who wants it, who spends it, who earns it, who lost it, who's angry, who's hurt, and who's responsible. Life is much easier with partners who share similar values and goals about money, whose buying and spending patterns match rather than clash.

It's double trouble when one partner believes that you can never be too rich, and the other believes that you already have plenty. It's triple trouble when money is scarce and partners can't agree how to make it, find it, keep it, or spend it.

Beliefs about money will override the numbers every time. When we compare ourselves to anyone richer than we are, we can feel like impoverished failures, deprived underachievers. When we compare ourselves to anyone who has less than we do, we can feel abundant, affluent, blessed, and really rich. Our estimate of our real wealth fluctuates, depending on where we put ourselves on the rich-to-poor scale.

Most TV shows and ads depict us as a nation rolling in wealth. There are few poor or financially strapped heroes in prime time. Families on TV usually have plenty of money. So it's easy to believe that we, too, should be living the easy, glitzy, affluent, good life. If we're not, we feel cheated and deprived. If our life doesn't look like theirs, if we're not Oprah or Donald Trump, if we don't have it all, what and who are we, really?

Creative advertisers feed our sense of inferiority by convincing us that we never have quite enough. Understanding the psychology of consumption is their passion. Luring us to choose their product, making it seem irresistible, is their art form. They're very good at what they do and they spend millions to get better. They study us to develop strategies that tempt us to buy into their version of the good life.

One strategy is to keep us just slightly out of fashion, just a little bit out of style, just barely out of sync with the latest trends. Every year, the top of the line changes somewhat. The shapes of cars and shoes change. The lengths of skirts and the widths of ties change. Computer software is obsolete as soon as we master it. We cannot keep up. Neither can anyone else. Kids laugh at our politically incorrect running shoes. Hackers deride last year's dinosaur computer. There's great pressure on all of us to stay new and shiny, fashionable and up-to-date, hip and up-to-code. The credit card companies know this and love it. But, in truth, the feel-good buzz doesn't even last long enough to pay off the interest on the balance. It's exhausting. And it's the American way.

Although we give lip service to the notion that money can't buy happiness, most people define success by wealth. If we could only afford the right stuff, all of our problems would be solved. Not true. Rich people have problems, too: the yacht needs repair, the stock market drops, the limo driver is unreliable, the upstairs maid is sleeping with you-know-who. It's hard to sympathize with the superrich, but the tabloids comfort us with weekly reminders that their internal worlds are as messy as yours and mine.

The American dream never includes complete instructions, so it's hard to tell when we've made it. Because there are no rules about what's enough money, fame, leisure, achievement, work, or education, no one ever feels complete, finished, satisfied, or able to rest. We rarely hear people say, "I've earned enough," "I've made it," "I don't need any more," or "I'm happy with what I have." It's easy to forget that most of us are far more affluent than most of the world.

In the beginning (Thin)

Just as we hardly ever believe we have enough money, we rarely believe we have just the right amount of flesh.

Weight has been an issue all our lives. From the moment we were born, people cared how much we weighed. They discussed whether we were big babies or small babies. They fretted over whether we were good eaters or fussy eaters. The doctor checked our weight against charts for normal, and we were defined early on by the numbers on the scale. Size mattered.

Size mattered even more when we got to school. Fat kids were teased unmercifully and chosen last for the team or for dates. Skinny kids were called weaklings and got sand kicked in their faces. The range of acceptability was narrow and is now narrower still. Most of us never even began to fit the ideal.

Now the pressure is so intense that even well-meaning parents urge their children to have perfect bodies, forgetting that the notion of perfect changes from generation to generation. They also forget that genes dictate how we look in jeans. Perfect for boys centers around fitness. Perfect for girls centers around appearance. Boys aren't expected to grow into thin men. Girls are expected to grow into thin women. Life is different for Ken than it is for Barbie.

In the present (Thin)

The ideal body keeps changing. Look at the changes in the shapes of presidents' wives, from Eleanor Roosevelt to Mamie Eisenhower to Jackie Kennedy to Nancy Reagan. Look at glamour photographs from the thirties, forties, and fifties, when women were appreciated for their curves. Now, women are appreciated for their angles and fashion models look like hungry, tall, adolescent boys. Every woman in America is convinced that to be acceptable she needs to lose at least ten pounds.

Although some cultures value weightiness as a sign of health and affluence, in this land of milk and honey, weight loss is a billion-dollar industry. Everyone is weight watching, measuring portions, and counting calories. Fat-free is America's mantra.

Narrow notions of acceptable body image cause many women to struggle with some form of eating disorder. They eat, feel guilty, take pills, diet, exercise, eat, throw up, feel guilty, diet, work out, feel better, eat again. Food becomes much more than simple nourishment. Food becomes a lover and an enemy, a companion and a nemesis, a preoccupation and an occupation, a reward and a punishment.

Food can also be used to deny and anesthetize strong feelings, to energize, to comfort, to diminish emptiness and loneliness. Unlike other feel-good drugs, food is necessary and inescapable. Eating is a daily event, a social event, even a special event. During the holidays, all the magazines at the checkout counter celebrate grog and eggnog, sweets and treats. As soon as the holidays are over, it's trimming and swimming, Lean Cuisine and dexedrine. What's a girl to do?

It's hard to feel satisfied with yourself when any womanly curve, bulge, or jiggle is defined as unsightly. Dimpled thighs have become ugly cellulite. Women need to "trim and flatten" for men with beer bellies. Men seeking women advertise, "No fatties need apply." Men on TV are permitted to have paunches and good tailors. Women on TV are punished or ridiculed for being too weighty, taking up too much space. Like older women, hefty women are not taken seriously. Both are used for comic relief. Thin is in. It's everywhere.

When girls and women feel most powerless and out of control, they can at least take charge of their bodies. They can play some version of the eat-now-pay-later game or the blame-the-body-and-punish-it game. They can lift weights to find definition. They can use laxatives and diuretics to lighten their load and push it to extremes.

Bulemics, feeling out of control, consume vast amounts of junk food and then throw up. They know all about instant gratification. Bulemics have bravely discovered how to eat everything and anything and not get fat. Like Wendy the compulsive shopper, they have repeated bouts of binging and purging. Rich and thin are two sides of the uncontrolled consumption coin.

Once upon a time

Wendy is a bulemic shopper. She has twelve credit cards. Most are charged to their limits. She needs two full-time jobs to make ends meet. She hungers for new clothes, even though her closets are overstuffed. She spends all her spare time in stores, checking out the latest styles. She buys everything she likes and puts it all on plastic. Finally full and satisfied, she goes home and unwraps her treasures. It feels like Christmas. She tries on all her new duds and parades in front of the mirror, never removing the tags. For this brief moment, she has it all. She is full and happy. But the buzz of satisfaction doesn't even last overnight. She wakes up the next morning feeling the consumer hangover—guilty, bad-tempered, and disgusted with herself. So she takes most of it back, credits her cards, and feels better until her hunger cycle begins again.

Wendy shops the way bulemics eat. She binges and purges and feels out of control most of the time. Wendy believes that when she has enough, she will be enough. When her outside self looks richly perfect, then her inside self will be content, relaxed, serene, cheerful, and good-tempered. She will never be satisfied.

Anorexics are never satisfied, either. Their version of the perfect body is so distorted that no matter how skeletal they are, they always see themselves as overweight. Their sense of self is bound up with controlling how they look. Ironically, these middle-class or upper middle class females have defined fat as their enemy. They will starve themselves to death rather than allow an extra pound on their frames. Although these eating disorders appear to be women's issues, they are a reflection of some of the culture's deepest values.

Some women at the other end of the scale from bulemics, anorexics, and fashion models use their weight to deny and subvert the Barbie stereotype. They refuse to accept the culture's definition of the attractive female body. Women sometimes use extra pounds to protect themselves from feeling too sexual, from being too vulnerable. Women who have been abused often hide their bodies under protective layers. Some women swallow their anger with their calories. Women sometimes want to be the "heavies," to feel substantive, weighty, and powerful, to take up space.

Now, more and more women are focusing on being healthy and fit, rather than unattainably skinny and fashionably perfect. Support groups are encouraging women to rethink their body image, to accept their genes, and to understand why eating has so much charge and drama in their lives. It's an endless battle to keep the culture's messages at bay. It's a struggle for women to refuse to be ashamed of their bodies, to stop torturing themselves, to quit trying to sculpt their flesh into stick figures they were never meant to be. How paradoxical that so much of the world is poor and hungry, and rich Americans choose to overconsume and starve.

Goal (Rich and Thin)

Wake up from the American dreams of money, sex, and power (the perfect portfolio), of thinness, sex, and power (the perfect package). Greed and overconsumption can kill you. Stop killing yourself.

Define your own dream, then figure out how to get from here to enough. Enough is never an absolute, never a fixed amount. Set your own limits. Be realistic. Decide what's right for you at this time in your life and under these circumstances. Question what your parents taught you, what the culture tells you, what the neighbors say, and what you see in the media. You have the last word.

Untie your self-esteem from your purse strings or your tape measure. You can be more than enough without having enough. You can measure up no matter what your measurements.

Stretch yourself

Here are some ideas for how you can get from here to enough.

Reshuffle your comparisons. Notice where you see yourself inside the American dream, whether you compare yourself to the Joneses next door, to the poorest person on the planet, or to the Trumps in the penthouse, at the top, in the middle, or at the bottom of the heap. There will always be others who have and weigh more than you do. There will always be others who have and weigh less than you do. Stop thinking vertically, defining yourself in terms of more or less. Try thinking horizontally, accepting rather than judging and comparing.

Notice how you consume. To buy or not to buy, to eat or not to eat, those are the questions. When you're out there in the trenches, ready to consume something to make you feel better inside, resist for ten minutes. Ask yourself, "Do I really love it?" "Do I really need it?" "Can I afford it?" "Will this really fill the void?" Wait and listen for the answers. You'll know what to do.

Redefine wealth. Wealth isn't just about money. It's about having a superrich life—full, varied, balanced, healthy, lively, and loving. You may already have a rich imagination, a magnificent mind, a bountiful personality, a splendid laugh, a resilient body, a worthwhile job, family and friends worth a million. Maybe you are rich enough already and just haven't noticed.

Remember the most satisfying times you had as a child. How much money did those times cost? How much did weight matter? Remember the most satisfying times you've had in the past five years. How much money did those times cost? How much did weight matter? Real satisfaction is almost never about size or money.

Enjoy never being too rich or too thin. Tolerate being successful in unusual ways. Cherish your peculiar and particular gifts. Get comfortable with having less, doing a lot with very little. Appreciate your flexibility and creativity. Honor your ability to live simply and with style. Often, less success means less stress, more fun with children and friends, doing the things you love to do. No one ever died wishing they'd spent more time at the office or on a diet.

Get comfortable with your body, your genes, the inevitable changes that happen over time. Look around. Be grateful for your health, your vitality, your uniqueness. Make friends with your shape, your size, your limitations. Talk to your body. Appreciate how well it functions. Respect its delicate balance. Enjoy its capacity for pleasure. Never punish it. If you must change your body, do it slowly, gently, with kindness and love.

Define your own dream of success. It might be very different from the American dream. Determine how much is enough for you, so you'll know when you've made it. Consider how much of your success depends on what you have or how you look, and how much depends on who you really are.

Be grateful for all you have.

Imagine what your life would be like if you were fat and poor and happy.

Affirmations

I won't risk my life for a smaller body and a bigger bank account.
I am already rich enough and thin enough.
I am worth more than I'm worth.
I matter more than my bankbook or my size.
I can handle money in ways my family never imagined.
I love and respect my body just the way it is.
I am grateful for what I have.
Right now, I am satisfied and content.
I am just the size I was meant to be.
I'm broke; therefore I am.
I eat; therefore I am.

18

Girls Are Made of Sugar and Spice?

Myth

Girls are made of sugar and spice and everything nice.
Girls are by nature sweet, cheerful, nurturing, tender,
and sensitive to the needs of others.

Truth

No one is that nice. Girls are also made of jumpy frogs, slimy snails, and puppy dogs' tails.

Raised to be sweet, it's not easy for most women to acknowledge or accept their frogs and snails, their power, or their darker sides. How can women be fully female, fully human, sugar and snails, frogs and spice, and still be okay?

Messages come at girls from all directions, telling them how to be female. Sometimes the images are subtle, like the pictures in schoolbooks that show boys having outdoor adventures and girls doing indoor things, wearing aprons, and being helpful. The boys look like they're having fun climbing trees and exploring. Girls look like they're having fun staying safe and clean and helping with dinner. Girls learn to tie bows. Boys learn to tie knots.

Before adolescence most girls can freely cross the gender line. When they're bored with paper dolls and tea parties, they can hang up the frilly lace dress, put on torn old blue jeans, tumble in the grass, and run with the boys. Tomboy is her name, adventure is her game. At puberty, most girls learn to give up boy games, take on more conventional roles, and do what's expected of them.

Through movies, books, school, church, TV, ads, and the rest of the stuff of life, we all learn the stereotyped differences between girls and boys. The way we talk about people is loaded with judgments about the nature and value of each gender. Such gender language is so commonplace that we often don't even notice it.

Females are described as:	Males are depicted as:
emotional	stable, grounded
dependent	independent
frail	strong
excitable, irrational	analytical, rational
unpredictable	logical, objective
submissive	dominant
responsive	self-starting
victims	heroes, saviors
passive	active
manipulative, covert	honorable, forthright
cooperative	competitive
childlike, vulnerable	mature, grownup, self-sufficient
nurturing, motherly	ambitious, adventurous
warm-hearted	cool-headed
ruled by unpredictable raging hormones	ruled by strong natural sex urges

A healthy person in this culture is historically defined as one who embodies so-called male traits. Traits perceived as female have been considered ineffective and undesirable in the worlds of decision making, high finance, and technology. Even our most ordinary language plays a role in determining how both men and women see women.

Girls Are Made of Sugar and Spice?

The usual terms for "human beings" ignore women by not naming them. "Man" is supposed to mean everyone. "Woman" does not mean everyone. Both men and women are supposed to be included in collective nouns like "mankind" and "cavemen." Women are missing even in "All men are created equal." Studies show that only men, not women, are visualized when common generic male terms are used. Notice what images appear when "mankind" is replaced by "womankind," or "cavemen" by "cavewomen." Would "All women are created equal" include men?

Consider the powerful differences between "master" and "mistress," "lord" and "lady," "sir" and "madam," "stud" and "slut." These and other common language usages leave girls feeling diminished, left out, disenfranchised, and envious. This could be what Freud really meant by "penis envy." When the language devalues women, women learn to reject and disdain themselves. Other females seem to be silly, irrelevant, unnecessary, and nothing more than rivals for men's affection. It takes some consciousness-raising for women to value themselves and other women as much as they've learned to value men.

Questioning and changing the language are signs that the good old predictable days of the patriarchy are waning. Some say it all went to wrack and ruin when women got the vote, got jobs, got degrees, got their own money, and got some power. Some say it only improved when women's voices began to be heard. Women no longer settled for being sex objects or just sweet desserts—honey bun, sweetie pie, sugar plum, cookie, candy, muffin, or sweetheart. They became a force to contend with, the whole enchilada, the main course. As women got bigger slices of society's pie, they were no longer willing to be little— baby, chick, kitten, pussycat, doll. They now insist on being called "women," not "girls" or even "ladies."

Changing language means that roles and opportunities are changing. Now women are struggling with glass ceilings. They are wrestling with being a working parent, with being taken seriously, with being seen and accepted as equal to, and different from, men.

In the beginning

Pregnant parents want to know if their new baby will be a boy or a girl.

153

If they learn this before the baby is born, they buy pink curtains or blue booties, dresses or baseball hats. One of the first things anyone says about us is, "It's a boy!" or "It's a girl!" Depending on our parents' values, our plumbing made us seem a blessing or a curse, valuable or merely tolerable.

Studies tell us that people talked to us differently if we were born male or female. They played different games with us, held us differently, told us we were pretty or smart, cute or strong. Sometimes our parents were more comfortable with one kind of plumbing than another. Sometimes our families were upset because our sex didn't meet their expectations. From all these implicit and explicit, positive and negative responses, we learned to feel good or bad about our sex. Peoples' attitudes about our sex taught us how to be in the world and established our gender. "Sex" is about our plumbing; "gender" is everything the world teaches us about our plumbing.

Early on, we learned:

"There was a little girl
Who had a little curl
Right in the middle of her forehead.
When she was good,
She was very, very good.
But when she was bad, she was HORRID!"

There was nothing in the middle for girls, no way to be anything between very good and horrid. Girls could be either Cinderella or the terrible stepsisters, Dorothy or the wicked witch of the west, Sleeping Beauty or the evil queen, a sweetie pie or a tart, virgin or whore—either one or the other, but never both.

Here's an example of how this works. From the story of *Snow White* we learn that ideal women are sweet, smiling, happy, nurturing. They are forever young, flawless, cheerful, helpful, pure, and virginal. In the story, Snow White's wicked stepmother, the terrible queen, wants Snow dead. The queen looks into the mirror and asks, "Mirror, mirror on the wall, who's the fairest of them all?" She is outraged to see Snow White's face in the mirror instead of her own. So she banishes Snow and asks a local huntsman to kill her. (Notice that the queen is old and angry and dark; Snow is young and cheerful and white.) The huntsman is unwilling to shed the blood of one so lovely. He frees Snow and lies to the queen, who believes her young rival is dead. The queen lives with this illusion until the next time Snow's image appears in her trusty mirror. The queen, once again, is more than a little displeased.

Meanwhile, back in the forest, Snow finds the seven dwarfs, each with his own special flaw, and joyfully takes up housekeeping. They establish a traditional family, where the female cheerfully does all the housework and the males go off to the diamond mines. They come home to swept floors, a cooked meal, and cheerful songs. Life's roles are divided along gender lines, and everybody's whistling while they work.

The evil queen finds Snow and, disguised as a vile crone, offers her a poisoned apple (think Garden of Eden). Snow bites and seems to die. The dwarfs are devastated. Unwilling to let her go, they place her pristine body in a glass coffin. They weep, but she remains unconscious—snoozing and waiting, snoozing and losing. Because this is a fairy tale, we anticipate that someday Snow's prince will come.

Sure enough, the handsome prince arrives and trips over the glass coffin. He is smitten with Snow's beauty, takes her into his arms, does the Heimlich maneuver, dislodges the poison apple, kisses her dead (but ruby red) lips, and—voilà!—she awakens instantly, alive and in love. The birds sing; the dwarfs dance; the sun shines in Mudville once again. The world is filled with romance and magic. There's no need for further discussion. Snow White and the prince will marry and live happily ever after.

And, pray tell, what profound lessons, might we learn from this story?

1. It pays to know the Heimlich maneuver.
2. Girls must stay forever sweet, young, and beautiful.
3. Old women are not to be trusted, especially if they're pushing apples.
4. Old queens and stepmothers can get really jealous and vengeful when they're replaced by younger and more beautiful women.
5. Good girls must cheerfully take care of all the men in their lives, even if they're grumpy, sleepy, sneezy, or dopey.
6. Good girls smile and whistle while they do housework.
7. True love comes only to girls who never get angry, grow old, or complain.

8. If you are perfect enough, someday your prince will come, especially if you seem dead.

9. Be patient. Be beautiful. Do nothing. Preserve yourself in glass. He will find you, give you the kiss of life, and carry you off into the sunset to live happily ever after.

In the present

Real life demands more of women than the Brothers Grimm could have imagined. Most contemporary women grow up to live unexpectedly demanding and challenging lives. They learn very quickly that it's both unhealthy and undesirable to spend time lying around in glass coffins, waiting to be rescued. The old stories don't work anymore, if they ever did, and most women are struggling to find new myths that are more relevant and less grim.

As the line between male and female behavior blurs, women ask:

"Is it really all right to rise out of my glass coffin and ask the prince for a date?"

"Can I really say that I don't want to cook dinner for the dwarfs every night? Could I ask them to cook dinner for me?"

"How can I tell a powerful older woman that I don't want to compete with her?"

"Can I ride my own horse alone into the sunset and still live happily ever after?"

"How can I be with a prince and still be the princess of my own queendom?"

These are daring questions for women who were raised to be the power behind the throne, the little woman, the housewife and mother who keeps the home fires burning bright and sacrifices her own needs for others. Women's roles have changed so much and so quickly in the last thirty years that no one is certain how to be a good woman anymore. Nowadays it's clear that women need more than sweetness, sugar, and spice to enter and survive in a fast-paced world that values putting yourself first, being competitive, earning big bucks, taking charge, and having it all.

Today mere girls like Snow White are being told to go to college, have careers, fulfill their potential, and also look like Barbie dolls, marry, care for a family, and run the PTA. The old roles and messages haven't been replaced; they've only expanded. It's not easy for a woman to live in the larger world and see herself as a prince of a woman without feeling like Snow White, a flake, or the wicked queen.

Alas, even today, princely women are often perceived as wicked. Women bosses can be despised for acting like men bosses. "Bitchiness" in women is called "tough-mindedness" in men. Where women are called "domineering," men are called "assertive." Women "demand"; men "ask." Women are "picky"; men "attend to details." Women are "gossiping and wasting time" when they gather around the water cooler and girl-talk about families. Men are "taking a well-deserved break and team building" when they boy-talk about sports.

Men are never seen as sleeping beauties or wicked witches. They're socialized to be awake and strong, to be more than they are: "Go for it!" "Reach for the stars!" "Climb right to the top." "You can do it!" Women are taught to be less than they might have been: "Be careful." "Don't be too pushy." "Don't hurt anyone's feelings." "Don't let anyone down."

Boys are taught to compete, strive, and win; girls are taught to cooperate, compromise, and not care about winning. Men and women even respond to success differently. Men think they've earned status; women think of themselves as just lucky. It's no wonder that even a queen with a Ph.D. can feel uncertain how to be a female mover and shaker. Even the most successful woman can feel like a fraud just waiting to be exposed.

This is a transitional and expansive time, and both men and women are muddling through it. Women are becoming more fearless and visible in the world. They're learning to cherish the most powerful and imaginative parts of themselves. They're becoming celebrated writers, scholars, historians, artists, politicians, doctors, jet pilots, weightlifters, and electricians. They're challenging the common wisdom. They're sharing more power with men as partners, friends, and colleagues, and adding variety to traditional models. The options are no longer limited to boy-way or girl-way, my way or your way.

Now every girl-princess has to decide how to be female *and* powerful, gentle *and* strong, caring *and* independent, nurturing *and* free, mother *and* career woman, breadwinner *and* bread baker. We're all stretching into new ways of thinking and being, beyond sugar, beyond spice, beyond nice.

Goal

Honor the whole emerging woman—imperfect and multifaceted. Remember, real diamonds have real flaws; only the fakes are perfect.

Honor the courage it takes to be a leader in the midst of gender upheaval.

Honor the jumpy toads, slimy snails, and exuberant tails within.

Honor the confusion that is bound to come with gaining and expanding consciousness.

Honor women; they hold up half the sky.

Stretch yourself

Make friends with the frogs and snails within; they can be sources of power and fun. Encourage them in others.

Explore yourself as Swampwoman, your new internal superhero. Give her a name. She's at home with dirt, dances with snakes, and calls a toad a toad. Swampwoman can be as sweet as Superman, as caring as Spiderman, as nurturing as Batman, as gentle as Tarzan. Let her roar! She's not afraid to be kind to creatures in need or to those who touch her heart. She's not afraid to flex her muscle or speak her mind. She's a real woman, made of sugar and snails, spice and nails, everything fierce and loving.

Choose when and where to unmask and reveal the Swampwoman within. This takes practice. You know who's ready (or not) to glimpse a whisker, a shining scale, a fang, or to hear a throaty growl, a war whoop, or an unexpected "no."

You might want to welcome more folks into your inner jungle. It's not very different from theirs. We have all been awakened in the dead of night by the call of the wild, parrots flitting through the palm trees and monkeys cavorting overhead. You are not alone. We are all Swampwomen underneath.

Affirmations

Good-bye Snow White. Hello frogs and snails.
I am female, powerful *and* vulnerable.
I'm full of surprises.
I'm more than sugar and spice and everything nice.
I'm Swampwoman as well as Snow White.
I have better things to do than play dead and wait.
I am both female and male; therefore I am.

19

Boys Are Made of Frogs and Snails?

Myth

Boys are made of frogs and snails and puppy dogs' tails. Boys are by nature strong, active, competent, productive, and independent.

Truth

It's a well-kept secret, but men and boys are also made of sugar and spice and everything nice under their jumpy frogs, slimy snails, and exuberant puppy dogs' tails. Men often feel frightened, inadequate, confused, self-conscious, weak, and vulnerable, just like women. The culture rarely allows them to acknowledge, accept, or show the sweetest and tenderest parts of themselves, however, or the darker emotions under all those manly disguises.

Girls are sometimes allowed and encouraged to be like boys, but boys are never allowed or encouraged to be like girls. It's shameful for boys to be caught playing girl games, to be sissies or wimps. But to be complete, men need it all, the female as well as the male, the full range

161

of feelings. It takes courage and imagination for men to fight the system and be fully male, fully human, sugar and snails, frogs and spice.

In the beginning

All human embryos begin life as female until the genetic code insists that some become male. When the newborn infant is wrapped in a pink or blue blanket, it's also wrapped in generations of social and cultural values and definitions. Like it or not, these blankets were woven long before any of us were born. Some threads comfort, others itch, and their patterns are slow to change. "It's a boy!" sounds like "It's a blessing!" to folks who value boys over girls. Boy babies give some families a sense of pride, identity, and continuity.

In days of yore, boys carried the family name and were revered as princes. It was assumed and expected that male heirs would grow up to take over the kingdom or the farm, help with the hard work, and become a source of pride and financial security for their aging parents. Girls were often seen as a drain on the family's resources. As a legacy of the old dowry system, the father of the bride still pays for the wedding. But now both boys and girls can earn degrees in agriculture, run the farm, and become a source of pride to the family. Both are equally able to provide financial security and care for their aging parents.

The old assumptions are all being questioned as science explores which gender differences are genetic and which are learned. But whether nature or nurture, some differences are obvious. Boys are usually bigger than girls. They more often build towers and play with trucks and guns. Girls tend to build circles and play house. Boys are more rambunctious, physical, and aggressive. Girls develop faster, both verbally and physically. Girls play more cooperatively. Boys play more competitively. Girls are taught to value relationships. Boys learn to focus on tasks and accomplishments.

Studies indicate that mothers speak more to their infant sons than to their baby daughters. Fathers are more physical and can be more punitive with sons. Families often have great expectations of their boys, sometimes demanding the impossible. They can weight down their sons' shoulders with their own imperfections and unfulfilled dreams—a heavy load for small boys.

Boys Are Made of Frogs and Snails?

Growing boys often seem related to frogs, snails, and puppy dogs' tails as well as to slime, snakes, and toads. They learn to show their prowess and fearlessness by putting the worms on fishhooks, embracing horror (plastic shrunken heads) and grossness (rubber vomit). They joyfully display their agility and flex their muscles. They love to show off, scare girls, shock adults, prove how invincible they are. Remember Tom Sawyer strutting his stuff for Becky Thatcher? It's an old guy story.

Boys see themselves as adventure seekers. They identify with Huck Finn, He-man, Spiderman, Batman, Superman, Indiana Jones, a Power Ranger, cowboy, or sports hero—more than human, larger than life, stronger than strong. They long to overpower, outsmart, and overcome all obstacles to reach the goal (posts). They strive to demolish evil and evildoers. They dream of being fearless, invulnerable, of saving the day, the world, and the damsel in distress.

From *Robin Hood*, young boys learn that the ideal guy lives with other guys, in the woods, outside the suburbs and the law. He is brave, athletic, mischievous, self-reliant, smart, fun-loving, and cunning. He's a handsome renegade leader, an outlaw, a hood who can't be captured or defeated, not anything like a girl. He is an unbeatable archer and a fearless horseman. He is noble, stealing from the rich and giving to the poor. He undermines the wicked authority of the sheriff and is loyal to his king. He is adored by a maiden and he performs impossible feats for her. All his friends admire him.

What profound lessons do we learn from this story?

1. It pays to be a good camper, marksman, trickster.
2. Never get old or let your green tights sag.
3. Never trust authority.
4. It's okay to steal, if you can convince yourself it's for a good cause.
5. Good men rescue and protect lovely ladies.
6. Real fun means belonging to a gang, hanging out with the guys, and bending the rules.
7. Never show signs of weakness or self-doubt.
8. If you are perfect enough, able to perform, provide, and protect, you will live happily ever after.

It's not so easy to be Robin Hood, Peter Pan, a prince, a warrior, and an outlaw when you're only a real live boy.

In the present

The romance of those old adventure stories lives on. The tales are so appealing, simple, and seductive that many men are still trying to live in some version of Robin's world. They invent their own rules, play their own games, and love to outsmart authority. In movies, real red-blooded American men are identified with power. They don't eat quiche. They beat drums. They are deceptive, heartless, ruthless, and shrewd. They never reveal plans or feelings. Mystery is mastery. They take the law into their own hands, trounce the opposition, and finish first. They always end up on top, both in the world and in relationships.

Real life requires more of real guys than Robin could have imagined. Real men are often allergic to pollen and small creatures in the woods. They may be uncomfortable in tights, unable to stay constantly on top of the day, the world, or the damsel in distress. They often see themselves as failures. It's hard for men to feel okay when they're less than the Lone Ranger, John Wayne, Captain Kirk, Jean-Luc, Rambo, Joe Montana, Babe Ruth, or Michael Jordan. The more they try to be Robin or Superman, the more they're reminded how Clark Kentish they really are. Some are relieved that they don't have to leap tall buildings, tote a machine gun, or live in the woods in winter. Those who feel they can't ever measure up often overcompensate and become prone to isms—workaholism, Don Juanism, alcoholism, working-outism, sports fanism, perfectionism.

Most men choose to grow up, be responsible, meet unexpected demands, and find new myths that include the realities of contemporary life. Men who accept being merely mortal can more easily share power without feeling powerless, live with losses without feeling like a loser, accept failures without feeling like a failure. They can separate what they do from who they are. Outside the movies, beyond Sherwood Forest, and off the playing field, everyone is a little heroic and a little wimpish, wins a few, loses a few, and mostly muddles through somewhere in the middle.

Boys Are Made of Frogs and Snails?

Some men embrace the powerful, heroic roles they inherited. Some question them. Some integrate the female parts of themselves. Many are still wandering in the woods, wondering how to be a playboy and a working man, how to live in the wilds and own a home, how to seduce maidens and be married, how to raise children and raise hell. Nothing is as simple and straightforward as it once was.

As women's roles have expanded, so have men's. Nowadays, birthing involves fathers as well as mothers, and raising children is no longer just women's work; it's everyone's work, just like going to the office. Today's maidens, enjoying challenges that Maid Marian never dreamed of, often don't need or want to be rescued, and refuse to be on the bottom. What's a guy to do when he can't use the old model or the old skills, and the old rules of power no longer apply?

One thing is clear: real men need more than frogs and snails and puppy dogs' tails to be fully human. Every man has to decide how to be male and vulnerable, strong and gentle, independent and caring, free and nurturing, both worker and father, breadwinner and bread baker. The old, inherited male model is continuously challenged. It's a time of expansion and we're all stretching into new ways of thinking and being.

Goal

Honor the whole man—imperfect and multifaceted. Real guys, like real diamonds, have real flaws; only the fakes are perfect.

Honor the courage it takes to be a leader in the midst of gender upheaval.

Honor the sugar and spice within.

Honor the confusion that is bound to come with gaining and expanding consciousness.

Honor women as well as men; each holds up half the sky.

Be all of who you are. An old Hasidic story tells us that when the venerable and beloved Rabbi Zusiah was dying, surrounded by his many students and disciples, one of his students asked, "Rabbi, aren't you afraid that when you die and go to heaven, God will ask you, 'Zusiah, in your long lifetime on earth, why weren't you more like Moses?'" Zusiah smiled and replied, "I'm much more worried that God will ask, 'Zusiah, why weren't you more like Zusiah?'"

Challenge the old, constricting patriarchal myths. Develop new models. Encourage flexibility.

Imagine being more cooperative and less competitive. The old win-or-lose approach works at the poker table, in sports, and sometimes in business, but rarely in close relationships. Competition and intimacy make strange and unhappy bedfellows. In a competition, every time someone wins, someone loses. Whoever loses will not be your best friend or lover or relative or intimate when the game is over. Aim for a win-win approach where everyone ends up satisfied and everyone finishes on top.

Cherish kindness and everything nice in yourself and others.

Stretch yourself

Make friends with the sugar and spice within; they can be the sweet Oreos of your soul.

Engage the most compassionate and generous parts of yourself. Cultivate patience. Start small.

Practice being a generous driver by imagining that every driver on the freeway is on your team. They're all wearing the same sweatshirts, and they're all trying to get somewhere, just like you. Leave your anger and impatience at the on ramp. Don't try to change or run over the world or other team members. Be especially kind to little old ladies who drive too slowly. Try smiling when another member of the team comes in first.

Experiment with losing and not feeling like a loser. Getting an F doesn't mean you're a failure; it's only information that you need to do something different the next time.

Practice letting someone else have the last word. Let them do something their way at their pace in their own unique style. You are not diminished when someone else does it differently and well.

Find ways to serve.

Laugh a little.

Laugh a lot.

Affirmations

Good-bye Robin Hood. Hello spice.
I'm more than frogs and snails and tails.
I can be hardheaded and softhearted and still be a man.
I'm more than any masculine mask I wear.
Once I was a sweet and vulnerable child. I still am.
I can let someone else lead.
When we play doctor, I can be the nurse.
I can take care of myself by asking for help and even for directions.
I am both male and female; therefore I am.

20

Old Patterns Lead to New Results?

Myth

If I do the same thing over and over again,
I will get new and different results.

Truth

If what you're doing hasn't worked the last 4,976 times, chances are it won't work the next 4,000 times, either. If you use a pitchfork to shovel the snow off the driveway, you'll end up with a snowy driveway. Using the same pitchfork next time won't work, either. Right job, wrong tool. Simple logic should confirm this truth, but not so. This myth isn't about logic, it's about hope, faith, perseverance, and being really hard-headed. This myth is about longing for the leopard to change its spots, for the elm tree to bear peaches, for fresh water to come from a dry well, for the brick wall to crumble, for other people to become miraculously changed and perfect.

Some realities are nonnegotiable. Some things or people won't ever change, despite our determination, loyalty, commitment, or stubbornness. Expecting something to be different doesn't make it so. Things are what they are. People are who they are. Wanting the planet to spin in a different orbit just doesn't work. Wanting people to be different just doesn't work. We can't make those things happen, no matter what we do. The sun won't rise one second before its time. All things behave according to their own natures and move according to their own timetable. The trick is to know when to stop trying to make things different, when to give up, when to let go, when to do something else. That's easy to say, but not so easy to do. It's rarely easy to admit our effort isn't getting us anywhere, and it's hard to quit trying.

In truth, some circumstances require hanging in beyond all mortal reasonableness, like climbing Mount Everest, practicing the piano concerto for the recital, working for social justice, or pushing hard toward any attainable goal. "Attainable" is the key word in that sentence. Consider the goal you've been struggling and straining and pushing and pulling for. Is it really attainable? Are the years of toil, blood, sweat, and tears worth it? Do you need a magic wand? What's the hard evidence that it can be done? Are the odds one in a million, one in a hundred thousand, one in ten? Get real. Given the odds, would you take this bet?

In the beginning

Children arrive on the planet innocent and hopeful. Their world is small and everything seems attainable. They believe in magic and think magically. They invent invisible friends, dig holes to China, look for four-leaf clovers, flap their arms and practice flying. They pretend to be dinosaurs, princesses, doctors, wild things. They search for the pot of gold at the end of the rainbow, stay awake until the stuffed animals are asleep, see ghosts and monsters in the closet, put out cookies and milk for Santa. For children, anything seems possible. After all, Uncle Lou can make silver coins come out of his ears.

Once, we all knew magic words and gestures. If we repeated those formulas often enough, surely something wondrous would happen. Repetition was the magical activity. We jumped off the bed over and over again, hoping to get airborne. We said "abracadabra" a hundred times and waited for the dog to turn into a unicorn. Although the dog was forever hornless, we remained undaunted. We persisted in believing we had the power to change things. It didn't matter that we had a small failure with the dog. We still had the power to change some things. If our baby sister stopped crying when we gave her a bottle, surely we could adjust the universe. Today, my sister; tomorrow, the world.

We also believed our dreams would come true if only we did the right thing. If we did the dishes well and often enough, our parents would be happier and stop yelling. If we mowed the lawn perfectly every week, fed the cat every day, smiled enough, looked happy enough, our mother or father would stop drinking. Small as we were, we passionately wanted to believe we had the power to change the adults in our world. That's magical thinking.

Growing up meant getting more realistic information about the limits of the known universe. Reality entered, stage left. We began to learn when we had power and when we didn't, when we could be wizards and when we couldn't. We learned that human bodies just aren't designed for flight. We learned that being responsible, reliable, and well-scrubbed changed nothing. No matter how often we did the right thing, we couldn't stop our parents from doing things we hated. No magic formula could be repeated often enough to change our world.

But kids thrive on repetition and find predictability comforting. They feel a sense of structure and security in the world to have milk and cookies before bed every night, to have pancakes or bagels every Sunday morning. Repetition is the royal road to mastery for kids. They build the tower of blocks a hundred times before they make it stand. They practice tying their shoes, writing their names, throwing a ball, singing the alphabet, and chanting multiplication tables. We all learned to try and try again until we got it right.

Sometimes we got it right, and sometimes we got it wrong. Repetition failed us when we tried over and over to get the new baby brother taken back to the hospital, or used sensible techniques for impossible tasks, like digging to China with a spoon, like dancing to make daddy wake up and pay attention. When we didn't land on the shores of the Yangtze River, when we didn't get asked for an encore, often we didn't question the tool or the task. Instead, we questioned and doubted ourselves, our abilities and our perseverance. Maybe if we had used a soupspoon instead of a teaspoon . . . Maybe if we had done one more pirouette . . .

In the present

Grownups still love magic and long for happy endings. That's what keeps us buying lottery tickets, betting on the underdog, playing bingo, and being finalists in the Publisher's Clearing House Sweepstakes. Somebody has to win, and it just might be you, or me, or us. Alas, it's usually the other guy who wins, and he doesn't deserve it nearly as much as we do. Members of Gamblers Anonymous are renowned for believing, "It could be me next time"; "I was so close"; "Just one more try, then I'll quit." This dream of success, wealth, and perfect luck is the golden karat that lures us to Las Vegas, makes bookies rich, keeps horses in the loading gates and magazines in our mailboxes.

Very clever entrepreneurs know how to keep us in love with Lady Luck and keep us coming back for more. They spend millions hiring the best behaviorists to apply the latest trends in motivational psychology. They play and prey on our delight in magic, luck, and happy endings. They learn their seductive tactics from their laboratory hero, Randy the Rat. Little Randy wants to be a big winner, too. He learns that when he pulls the lever he gets a food pellet. He likes that. In lab rat language, it's called "positive reinforcement." Randy is trained to expect his delicious reward. Pull the lever and, yum, dinner.

Then those crafty behaviorists change the rules without telling Randy. He keeps pulling the lever, but the pellet now only appears at random. Randy doesn't understand this, and it makes him a little crazy. He thinks (like we do), "If I just keep pulling that lever over and over again, the food pellet I want will surely drop out. It did once. It will again. I'll push a little harder, over to one side, a little softer, a little faster, a little slower. Where is my pellet? I must be doing something wrong." Randy is ready to give up. He becomes as confused as we are. "Why does it work sometimes for some rats and not for me? I'm as good a rat as the rest. I keep trying and trying and trying. Where is my dinner?" Suddenly another pellet drops and the cycle begins again. In lab rat language, this is called "intermittent reinforcement," and it's seriously addictive.

Randy and his rat friends taught Las Vegas all about intermittent reinforcement. It really works. Slot machines keep us pulling the lever until our arm nearly separates from our shoulder. They are designed to be irresistible. They tease us into believing (like Randy) that if we stay up all night, pull the lever just one more time, harder, quicker, slower, gentler, magic will happen. Three cherries! Three bells! Three lemons! The jackpot! The IRS!

Intermittent reinforcement in the lab, in Las Vegas, and in our living rooms keeps us hopeful, hooked, and hopeless. In our living rooms, we do relationships just the way we do slot machines. We believe that if we just hang in there, just keep playing (harder, quicker, slower, gentler), we will eventually win and our lemon will turn into three cherries. Intermittent reinforcement keeps us having the same argument over and over in slightly different ways, hoping to get different results. It keeps us in terrible relationships, hoping and trying to make the other person change. We beg, plead, and nag, urging our partners to become the great people they were really meant to be. We fall in love with their potential, with the promise of the grand-slam jackpot, with our visions and dreams of the perfect win. Like Randy, we stay loyal and stuck.

And, like Randy, when we don't win the jackpot, we believe there must be something wrong with us, not something wrong with the situation. We believe that if we stop now, the next rat to pull the handle will get the goodies and the benefit of all our persistence. They win. We lose. It is easy to imagine that our imperfect ex-spouses are now perfect with their new mates. They miraculously change into the people we always wanted and knew they could be if only we had tried harder.

Once upon a time

Joan and Bill, her ex, had been everyone's perfect couple. It was true. They'd had many friends, shared similar politics, interests, and tastes, and were cheerfully building a wonderful life together.

After four years of wedded bliss, things began to change. Bill started working late, sleeping late, and making excuses to avoid sex. He said he was preoccupied with business, had headaches, was stressed by work, and couldn't talk about it. Joan grew concerned about his silence. She rubbed his back and was understanding. But things grew worse. He became angry when she wanted to talk, avoided intimacy, and refused her advances. She was puzzled by the disappearance of the loving, devoted husband she'd once known.

Joan wanted her marriage more than anything in the world and was determined to save it. Bill said he was confused, tired, and overworked. He asked for patience and understanding while he sorted things out. She agreed. That was the least she could do after all the wonderful years they had spent together.

So she waited. She understood. She watched for signs. She cried with him, about him, and for him. She went to therapy. She went to an astrologer. She quietly raged. She threatened. She talked to him and listened to his silence, looking for clues. As the tension grew, so did her alarm. She knew she must be doing something wrong. She tried and tried to make it right. She lost weight. She bought sexy nightgowns. She cooked gourmet meals. She even washed his car. Nothing seemed to work. He didn't seem to notice or care behind the plexiglass wall he'd built around himself.

It was a year before Joan let herself discover the truth. She'd never imagined that there could be another woman, but it turned out that he was having an affair with his secretary. Joan told herself that something essential was missing in herself. Some big flaw had sent him elsewhere.

Joan persisted. She could wait for Bill to come to his senses and return to her. Surely he would get this out of his system. Joan read books. She redecorated. She got her hair styled. She grieved. She threw tantrums. She pleaded for marriage counseling. She threw him out. She let him back in. She left home. She came back. She tried everything her friends, her therapist, and the self-help books suggested. Nothing worked.

Another year went by and Bill didn't change one bit. He said he was mixed up, undecided, having a midlife crisis. He wanted the marriage and he wanted his other woman. Joan tried, but she couldn't live with that. She was running out of strategies, running out of hope, running out of energy to keep playing the slot machine of her marriage.

Finally Joan went next door to a neighbor who had been divorced for many years. She told her story, wept, and asked, "When do you know you've done enough, tried enough, waited long enough? When do you know it's time to give up?"

The neighbor replied wisely, "If you have to ask the question, then you're not ready to let go."

It was true. Joan hung in there for another three months. Finally she realized that she wasn't going to win any jackpots here. No matter what she did, Bill was not going to be different. He wasn't going to give up his affair. He was never going to want the marriage she wanted. He wasn't going to choose. She had to let go. She couldn't change him and she couldn't make a marriage by herself. Feeling like a failure, she filed for divorce. One person giving 100 percent just can't substitute for two people each giving 50 percent.

It's not easy to stop hoping, to let go of a relationship or a one-armed bandit that's been swallowing all our time, energy, and money. If we quit now, we might just miss out on the perfect jackpot, the perfect payoff, the perfect life. The voices inside our heads shout: "Don't be a quitter, a loser, a doubter." "Try just a little harder for a little longer." "You can fix this." "Don't give up." It's tough to know when we've tried enough, lost enough, endured enough, hoped enough. It's really tough to know when to stop and let go.

Alas, no one can answer these questions for us. We have to listen to our own deepest wisdom to find our own best answers. We can listen to our bodies pleading with us to stop, rest, quit, let go. We can listen to the people who love us and want the best for us.

Or we can keep doing things the same way. And the outcome will be the same as it was every other time. Nothing will change until we do.

Goal

Try, try again, and if you don't succeed, stop. If you've tried this hard for this long and haven't gotten it yet, it may be time to let go. The serenity prayer says it best: "God, grant me the serenity to accept the things I cannot change, courage to change the things I can, and the wisdom to know the difference."

Stretch yourself

Imagine stopping the behavior you've been repeating over and over, hoping things will be different. You may feel bereft with no problem to occupy your time and energy. What will you do with yourself? If you stop going to a dry well for water, what will you do for exercise? If you and your friends agree to stop your endless and unproductive arguments, what will you do instead? If you abandon all plots and schemes to change your loved one(s), what else can you plot and scheme about?

When you're failing to change your universe, when all your tactics are unsuccessful, stop what you're doing. Seek help. Ask everyone you know for other ways to proceed. Your experience is not entirely unique, and the most unlikely people will often provide the most innovative solutions. Check in with the folks around you informally, or join a group like Al-Anon, ACoA (Adult Children of Alcoholics), Gamblers Anonymous, or Parents Without Partners, and listen to those who are struggling with the same issues. They'll understand, and may surprise you.

Move your thinking from, "If only I had . . . ," to "Next time I will . . . " Move from dreaming about how things should be different to focusing on practical next steps you can take. Take one.

Affirmations

I can quit without being a quitter.
I can lose without being a loser.
I can overcome intermittent reinforcement.
I can decide when to stop and when to let go.
I can change my mind.
I can't change other people.
I will not want more for others than they want for themselves.
I will not give up my day job to play the slots.
I succeed and I fail; therefore I am.

21

Do Everything Alone?

Myth

I should never need any help. I should be able to do everything alone.

Truth

Since the beginning of the world, never has anyone ever done everything alone. We all got help getting into this world, and we need lots of help getting through it. Batman had Robin. Cagney had Lacey. The Lone Ranger had Tonto. Even John Wayne had his horse.

In the beginning

Because we were human babies, we needed a lot of help for a long time. How we got that help taught us a lot about giving, receiving, and getting our needs met. Some babies felt important because their cries brought instant results. Some babies worried because there was no response to their cries and they didn't know how to get instant refills on their bottles. We may not consciously remember, but if we believed that no one was there for us, that we couldn't get help when we needed it, we may have learned not to ask for help, and we're still not asking.

When we got the care we needed, we felt that we had a perfect right to be in this world and ask for help. We could trust our caretakers, bond with them, separate from them, and still be okay. What we learned as children enabled us, as adults, to feel safe (or not so safe) being cared for. If we believed that we shouldn't want anything from anybody, we hid our needs from others and from ourselves, and soon we forgot that we had any needs. We were like the drowning person who said, "What, me? Need anything? I'm just fine. Really I am. Glug. Glug." Asking for a life preserver felt too shameful, too risky. We became rigidly independent and proudly treaded water for years. Some of us need a lifetime to learn that it's okay to want or need help, to be embarrassed, and to ask for it anyway.

Most kids start school eager to cooperate. They want to get an A in "works well with others." Too often, however, when they reach out to help a classmate, they're told that everyone needs to work alone. Helpfulness and cooperation are labeled "not working independently," or worse, "cheating." The unwritten rules say it's only okay to get help from the teacher, who is often overloaded, with enormous demands and limited time. So children learn that asking for help, or giving it or needing it, can be hazardous to their grades and their self-esteem.

In some families, asking for help was seen as a sign of weakness. Kids got these messages: "Just pull yourself up by your own bootstraps." "Be strong." "Figure it out yourself." "I'm too busy. Don't bother me." "You're so stupid!" In situations like these, children learned quickly how to hide their needs, ask for nothing, be independent, and leave home as soon as possible.

In the present

As creative grownups, we invent all kinds of imaginative tactics to avoid asking for help. We pretend to be the expert, to know it all. We change the subject, make jokes, use put-downs, sarcasm, or anger. We avoid new people, places, or ideas. These strategies harden into masks of competency that become difficult to peel off. People who fear losing face drive around in circles for hours unwilling to remove their masks and ask for directions. (You know who you are!) Masks also interfere with kissing. If we can't show our vulnerability or our neediness, it's nearly impossible to be intimate.

So there we are, walking around the house, wearing our masks and inventing a hundred reasons not to reach out and ask anyone for anything. "I could ask for help. . . . No, he's probably too busy. He's tired after work. I know he's not interested. His life is too full already. He'll probably say no anyway, so I'd better not ask." Or, "If I ask I might be imposing. . . . If she says yes I'll feel guilty. Besides, she only says yes because she's polite. She won't really mean it. I won't bother her. I'll just do it myself." We can scare ourselves into isolation. "I can do it. I don't need any help. I'll figure it out. No one will really help me, anyway. I don't want to intrude. It's dumb to ask for help. I don't want to look stupid. I'm not helpless. It's not that bad."

What would happen to us if we took off our masks and reached out? Who would see us? Who would bite us? If we just asked for what we wanted, we would look less than perfect. We might get new information that doesn't fit what we've always believed. We might have to rethink our most cherished assumptions. We might get a frightening yes. We might get bitten by the dreaded no. No doesn't inflict a mortal wound; it's only a (sometimes awful) disappointment. We eventually learn to live with it. And we do survive, just as we always have. Sometimes an unexpected no tells us something useful and even clears the air.

When we ask directly for what we want, a surprising number of people will say yes. Some will even appreciate being asked. Accepting a helping hand may feel humbling at first, but if we breathe deeply, it will get easier with practice. We always have a right to ask, the same right our friends have. Good timing helps. So does experience. Some people we know have been waiting years for us to ask them for something, anything. And sometimes, someone might say no.

Once upon a time

Joe was sitting in his freshman English class, understanding not a word the professor was saying about dangling participles. "I'm sure you all remember these from high school," the professor said. Joe hadn't been in high school for ten years and had no memory of ever meeting a dangling participle. Did they even have dangling participles back then? All these years, Joe had been at home, in the real world, raising his children. His only writing assignments had been notes to the kids' teachers and Christmas cards. Now he was beginning again, ready for more education, but English had never been his best subject. He was paying attention, taking notes, and still felt lost. He looked around the class and thought, "Everyone but me seems to be understanding this stuff. I must be the only dummy here. I'd better keep my mouth shut and figure it out for myself."

The professor was now traveling through noun clauses and other foreign territories. Joe was lost and longing for direction. He took a deep breath. Even if everybody else knew the terrain, he didn't. He swallowed hard, raised his hand, and, feeling like a fifth grader, asked the professor for clarification. The class heaved an audible sigh of relief. The professor looked around the room. "This is pretty difficult," he said. "Let me slow down and explain it another way." Some students stopped Joe after class and thanked him. They, too, had been lost and were too embarrassed to ask for help. (You know who you are.)

This story happens thousands of times every day in classrooms, board rooms, and living rooms everywhere. Folks tell themselves that they'll look like fools if they ask, so they don't.

There really is no such thing as a stupid question, and we have the right to ask anything of anyone. They can always refuse. And sometimes they will. Teaching and learning, like life, are cooperative ventures. We don't need to do it all alone.

Goal

Face it. You need help. You probably can't move the piano up the stairs by yourself or take out your own appendix. Let it be okay to be helpless sometimes. Learn to ask. Everyone does it. You can, too. If you're afraid that other people won't do things exactly your way, you're probably right. They're not you. They won't be perfect, either.

Give the universe the opportunity to say yes. It likes to do that.

Let yourself be a learner as well as a knower, a beginner as well as an expert, a receiver as well as a giver, an imperfect person as well as an occasional saint.

Stretch yourself

List your allies. Include the cat, the mailman, your best friend, your horse, your bookie, your broker, the librarian, your neighbor, your vet, your e-mail pals. They're all potential helpers, and they're already in your life.

Shock your friends. Say yes when they ask, "Can I help you?"

Practice cooperation and cultivate synergy. The Beatles together were far better than any of the four alone. Invite dialogue, discussion, brainstorming.

Transform a difficult solo project into a cooperative venture. Collaborate. Ask a person to do something with you—cook a meal, wash a car, read a poem, write a letter, help you move, garden, baby-sit. Asking for help gets easier with practice. Eventually you can get to half the anxiety and twice the fun.

Affirmations

I can choose not to do it all alone.
I can choose when to ask and when not to.
I am smart and I still need help.
I am strong and I still need help.
I am imperfect and I still need help.
I can handle a no.
I can handle a yes.
I can handle being embarrassed.
I am willing to be a beginner, a learner.
I need all the help I can get!
I ask; therefore I am.

22

To Know Me Is to Leave Me?

Myth

If you really knew me, you'd reject and abandon me.

Truth

The more strongly we dislike, reject, and abandon ourselves, the more we're convinced that others will do the same. The more we like and accept ourselves, the less we feel rejected or abandoned when someone tells us, "No, thanks." Let's face it, rejection cannot be avoided. Hide ourselves or show ourselves, people will say no to us, have other plans, turn us down, and leave before we want them to. We can label all of those behaviors and countless others as rejections.

Some of us are experts on rejection; we find it everywhere. We can feel rejected by the simplest act, by the slightest imaginary slight—when people don't answer the phone, when we get their answering machines, when they don't reply to our e-mail, when they've left town, when they don't wave good-bye, when they die. We can spend long mornings and endless afternoons feeling terrible about being abandoned. We can fill evenings and weekends reviewing our rejections, recounting them to friends, replaying them in our heads, writing them up in our journals.

Feeling rejected can be a full-time job. It can be used to affirm and bolster any and all of the negative feelings we have about ourselves. We can use rejection as proof positive that we are once again unlovable, unwanted, ugly, monstrous, too stupid, too smart, oversexed, undersexed, overweight, underweight, worthless, _____ (fill in the blank).

How different it feels when we are doing the leaving and rejecting, when we say no to someone, have other plans, turn them down, and leave before they want us to go. When we do the declining or leaving, we rarely feel as though we're rejecting. Almost always, the issue is not theirs; it's ours. We're not saying no because of them; we're saying no because of us. Our needs, desires, and priorities are only different from theirs. Rejection, like acceptance, is in the eye and mind of the beholder.

In the beginning

For a thousand unremembered reasons, sometime in the murky past we cast ourselves as the lead monster in a horror movie that still flickers at the back of our psyches. Over the years, we trusted only a lucky few to see it. We were amazed when they didn't find our monsters all that scary, didn't walk out in the middle, didn't judge us nearly as brutally as we judged ourselves, didn't even think of rejecting or abandoning us. Instead of being our worst critics, they were busy judging themselves, starring in the feature attractions and reruns showing inside their own heads, mesmerized by their own secret and slimy creatures. Everybody thinks their monster is the most uniquely unacceptable.

We were not born with a scary or depressing self-image. We were not born with any self-image at all. We first saw ourselves mirrored in the faces of those around us. And mostly we reflected back their moods, their feelings, their beliefs about us. Seeing ourselves through their eyes, we developed a sense of self and judgments about that self. Usually, we judged ourselves as we were judged, for better and for worse. Sometimes we didn't get the reviews we longed for, so we invented new, improved versions of ourselves to fit into the world and to avoid rejection and abandonment. Imaginatively we created ways to please our critics, to get raves, applause, and even Oscars for our performances.

By comparison, our original, internal, ordinary selves began to seem shabby and even shameful. We silenced those inner selves, judged them, hid them in the dark basements of our psyches and kept them a secret. Soon our inner selves grew into creatures that seemed crude, rude, and dangerous. We shunned them and banned them from the public eye. We held private showings only. Over time, and with plenty of practice, we became our own worst critics. We still are.

Children want to be reassured that even their darkest selves are not really threatening. They want a fan club, a cheering section, something like a public relations firm to remind them that although they're not perfect, they're certainly good enough to be on the big screen. Imagine if someone had called on the cellular phone attached to the bunk bed and said, "Hey, kid, look again. Maybe you're really all right, inside and out. No one's noticed yet that you're a great kid and a terrific talent. You're fabulous. There's never been anyone like you. You're star material." All children hunger for praise, appreciation, recognition, and acceptance of their real selves, especially as they become teenagers.

During the tumultuous years of adolescence, we tried to figure out who we were. We shifted our focus from our families to the larger world. We had to figure out all over again how to be accepted. We tried on other people's clothes and other people's personalities, looking for a good fit. We grew self-conscious and became obsessed with how we looked. We showered. We scrubbed. We groomed. We combed. We sprayed. We fussed. We prayed for clear skin and muscle definition. As our bodies changed, we worried more and more about less and less. Once again, others' reactions became our mirrors. We saw ourselves through their eyes and measured ourselves by what we imagined they saw.

Sad but true, too often our looks determined our popularity, our social standing, and our sense of success. Too often, depending on where and how we grew up, our brains, artistic skill, mechanical aptitude, musicianship, or other talents just didn't count. Some of us had many spotlights under which to shine. Some of us had few or none. We all learned everything about rejection. No wonder no one wants to be an adolescent again.

Pressure to look right came from our peers, and a lot of it came from other places, too. Media, media, media filled our living rooms and our psyches with images of idealized youth, the wealthy, the ever-so-cool, the tragically hip. Unlike us, they were all physically perfect. No media hero ever sported a zit or bad hair, extra weight, glasses, braces, a hearing aid, crutches, or a cane. As children or adolescents, if we were physically less than perfect (and all of us were), we probably suffered abuse, shame, and embarrassment in our search for acceptance.

No one ever told us (nor did we really want to hear) that each of our lifetimes will inevitably include periods of disability. No one reminded us that we are all only temporarily abled. Most of us are even now physically challenged in some ways most of the time. Some parts of us simply function better than others. And some parts of us, thanks to genes, experience, accidents, luck, and fate, are significantly less than perfect.

Unfortunately, a very large part of our self-image was manufactured during those lumpy, formative teenage years. Bad timing. Those were the years of hormonal upheaval, hourly identity crises, and continuous self-loathing. No wonder we felt inadequate, inept, scared, and completely unlovable. No wonder we kept falling desperately in love, longing for someone to discover the real us and love the monster within.

In the present

We've all been told that our consciousness is something like an iceberg. Our aware self is only one-tenth above water. It responds uncontrollably to the erratic currents beneath the surface. Our unconscious is like the underwater part of the iceberg; nine-tenths of our personality is submerged, inaccessible, and mysterious.

Our unconscious selves, the selves of our dreams and deepest imaginings, are often described as sinful, scary, needing to be tamed, trained, civilized, and domesticated. We can define our own unconscious selves as terrifying and hostile, filled with danger to ourselves and others. We can learn to be deeply ashamed, judgmental, and worried about the hidden parts of ourselves. After all, any part of us that lives underwater might just bob up to the surface at any moment, cause a major tidal wave, and flood the entire planet.

This iceberg model of personality contributed mightily to those old "Who am I?" movies we all made during childhood and adolescence when we established the definitive stories of who we really are. Those early fictions can become classics and affect us profoundly whenever we most doubt ourselves or feel most vulnerable.

Once upon a time

Dawn's husband, Chuck, had just left her for another woman. She felt like a failure, unloved and unlovable. She had revealed her deepest truths to Chuck, and now he had rejected and discarded her. The past seemed full of pain, the present felt full of anguish, and the future looked bleak, verging on hopeless. She scolded herself for having shared too much, for having been so open and trusting.

On the outside, Dawn was attractive, capable, solvent, successful. On the inside, she felt stupid, loathed her personality, hated her looks.

During her separation, many friends and caring coworkers were sympathetic and supportive. She was invited to lunch, taken to dinner, asked to parties. This made no sense to Dawn. She believed that if anyone ever discovered who she really was, they, too, would abandon her. Chuck knew her. He had left. Logically it followed that anyone who really knew her would flee. If Chuck didn't want her, no one would want her. Not now, not ever.

Dawn's phone continued to ring. Friends called to ask how she was feeling, eating, sleeping, doing. But Dawn's internal soundtrack was loud and shaming. Her friends' caring and concern sounded faint by comparison, muted and distant. She could hardly hear them.

One night, home alone and weeping, wallowing in despair and self-pity, Dawn found herself thumbing through a photo album. She came upon a picture of herself at sixteen in her baggy gym clothes, a skinny, freckled, gawky girl with frizzy hair. She'd felt like a failure then, too. Ashamed of her body, her confusion, her inadequacies, she never revealed her inner self to anyone. Instead, she put on a cheerful face and pretended to be perky. Inside her head, Dawn watched old reruns of herself from the archives of her most painful adolescent memories. Those awkward, lonely, and tortured years had seemed to go on forever.

Now, at 36, Dawn allowed herself a moment of enlightenment. She wiped her tears, blew her nose, and tried looking at the photo in the album with more grown-up eyes. Twenty years had passed, but no accomplishment, praise, or success, great or small, had revised her outdated autobiography. Her old adolescent feelings of despair and hopelessness had returned, resurrected by her lost marriage and impending divorce.

Chuck had seemed to love and accept the parts of her that she had most hated and abandoned, including that insecure, troubled sixteen-year-old girl inside. Now Chuck was gone. Left alone with herself and her outdated self-image, Dawn was feeling like a nerdy teenager once again. Still frozen in the past, like a woolly mammoth in a glacier, she was disconnected from the warm, competent, adult woman she had become.

For the first time ever, grown-up Dawn began to question her perceptions of herself. She had added her successes to her resume but not to her frozen identity. She wasn't skinny anymore, her hair wasn't frizzy, and her baggy gym clothes had long since disappeared. She'd shed that troubled sixteen-year-old skin long ago and hadn't ever acknowledged that she'd grown into someone else. Now she had to thaw out, discover who she was today, and move on into the adult life she'd created for herself. But she didn't have a new image in place and didn't trust her old perceptions.

Over the next few weeks, white-knuckled and queasy, Dawn asked her closest friends how they saw her. She braced herself to listen to their answers. Their vision of her was very different from her own. They were positive and appreciative. She was shocked that she had never seen herself as they saw her.

They knew her as she was now. They hadn't known her when she was sixteen. They hadn't judged her harshly for twenty years. Maybe Dawn wasn't a woolly mammoth after all. She began to let the good stuff in, even though it was terribly painful, like when frostbitten fingertips begin to thaw.

Dawn keeps that photo of herself in her mind, and she has lots of sympathy and appreciation for that young, awkward girl inside. The day even came when she could smile nostalgically at her old wedding picture, recognizing how hard it had been to let go and go on. She was no longer a gawky adolescent or a blushing bride. That was then; this was now: a new dawn.

Dawn's inner self felt like a teenage blobby nerd. Yours may feel like an alien, a creep, a dunce, a slimy green monster, a frightened child, or some combination of the above. It is hard to remember that these yukky parts of ourselves are not all of who we are. It's easy to forget that we do manage to fit into the grown-up world even when we still feel like children. We do make it in prime time even when we feel like a Saturday morning cartoon. We all spend a lot of our adult lives balancing our internal and external selves, who we thought we were then and who we really are now.

How we live with our self-image affects every relationship we have. When we dislike, doubt, and hide our inner selves, when we question our real worth, we wonder why anyone with any sense would choose to be with us. Groucho Marx said, "I don't want to belong to any club that would have me as a member." Woody Allen advanced this concept in films that glorify insecurity and self-doubt. Now we say, "I don't want to be with anyone who would have me as a partner." So we fake it. We step out there with our best foot, face, facade forward. We try to glitter and dazzle, hoping no one will notice the real us tripping over ourselves.

The sad thing is, when people fall for our elegantly constructed facades, deep down we are disappointed in their shortsightedness. If you fall in love with my gorgeous outside, how can I ever know or trust that you could love the real me? I can't. That's the heart of the Marilyn Monroe story: men kept falling in love with her manufactured showgirl. She killed herself believing that no one ever saw or knew or loved the real Marilyn.

Unfortunately, Marilyn was no fluke. Women are still taught that their looks are the most important thing about them. This may seem trivial, but it has serious consequences. When men lose their looks, they expect to be cared for and to have their inner lives valued. When women lose their looks, they fear that they will be rejected and abandoned for prettier pastures.

Once upon a time

Paula's car was broadsided at an intersection near her house. The accident left her with a disfigured face that plastic surgery could only partially correct. The stares of people she knew and didn't know left her embarrassed and exhausted. She found herself struggling with shame about her new face. Having been trained to keep all imperfections hidden, it was terrible to have the scars on her face all too visible. Her husband left their ten-year marriage, telling her he was sure she'd understand. She understood all too well. Paula became a recluse, hiding from a world that wouldn't see past her damaged exterior.

Paula's brother, worried about her isolation, bought her a computer and taught Paula how to get online. Soon she found herself communicating with people all over the world who couldn't see her and didn't care how she looked. Slowly she began to feel more alive, and remembered that she was far more than just a pretty face. She was amazed to find how many other women felt just as she did.

In her home town, Paula set up a support group for those who were coping with internal scars, shame, and disfigurement that no hospital had noticed.

Supported by her group, Paula got in touch with the local hospital and began talking first with nurses and then with doctors about the psychological pain of disfigurement. Soon she put together a presentation to help medical professionals understand the lonely and complex lives of their disfigured patients. Although her scars were still a source of anguish for her, they had catapulted her into a new and unexpected life with unforeseen challenges. Her anguish enabled her to access surprising talents, to establish a new and productive dialogue between her internal and external selves, and to share that dialogue with others.

Events that transform our lives—accidents, illnesses, deaths, divorces, relocations, career changes, children coming and going—often demand that we rethink who we really are and redefine the deepest layers of our identity. During these times of transition, we need far more than our ordinary ration of love, support, encouragement, and help.

Goal

Reframe the picture you have of yourself. You've changed. Nothing is permanent, not you, not your looks, not your identity, not your identity crises. You are not the same person you were ten years ago, or even ten days ago. Keep updating your image. Rewrite and tune out any destructive and tiresome stories you tell yourself.

Shorten the distance and differences between your inner and outer selves. Some people will accept and love you, no matter what. Some people will judge, reject, and abandon you, no matter what. You might as well let yourself be who you really are. Practice looking at your less-than-perfect self with your most grown-up and loving eyes. Let people love you.

Stretch yourself

Get new information about yourself from the people who care about you. Add it to your resume. Post it on your bulletin board. Store it in your internal hard drive.

Never let anyone criticize you. They may state their preferences, their opinions, and ask you to do things differently, but they are not allowed to be mean to you. That part of your life is over. If anyone dares to criticize you, don't take their judgments too seriously. Just ask what they would like you to do differently and move on. Separate comments about your behavior from comments about your character. You can choose to change behavior.

Never criticize yourself. You may state your preferences, your opinions, and ask yourself to do things differently, but you are not allowed to be mean to yourself. That part of your life is now over. When you hear your sneaky critical voice, turn it into the voice of Donald Duck. Lower the volume. Don't let any quack tell you what to do.

Be smart about when and where to share yourself, because not everyone will love you (their loss). There are situations when it's down-right dangerous to reveal the real you. People are punished every day for being different. They're branded for their politics, their religious beliefs, their sexual orientation, their level of literacy, their looks, their accents, their unusual choices. Everyone loses in this game. Choose when to hide in the closet and when to come out. Stay safe. Safe, non-judgmental people will make eye contact, listen to you, hear you. They will accept you, validate you, be direct, have clear boundaries, and be authentic with you.

If you insist on continuing to reject and abandon yourself, here are eight tried and true ways to get others to reject and abandon you, too.

1. Be cold. Never warm up to any relationship.
2. Be busy. Never have time or energy for anyone.
3. Be fast. Reject everyone before they reject you.
4. Be devious. Dodge. Weave. Pretend. Play hide-and-seek with anyone who really wants to know you. Don't let them find you.
5. Be invisible. Never let anyone see the real you.
6. Be scary. Be like all the people you most fear and dislike. Frighten everyone.
7. Be prophetic. Be certain that all relationships will end quickly and badly. See to it that this happens.
8. Be isolated. Suffer alone. Reject and abandon everyone who cares about you.

Now that you have successfully ended up alone, you might as well learn to be good company for yourself.

Teach yourself to appreciate solitude. When all is said and done, when the shouting and the crying are over, when the applause fades and the theater is dark, you'll be alone again. Get with the program.

Affirmations

I can love the monster within.
I never need to feel rejected or abandoned.
I never need to criticize myself.
The real me is the most vulnerable part of me.
I can make friends with the scariest parts of myself.
I can take myself to show-and-tell and not show or tell.
I can look at myself with grown-up eyes.
I'm the first charter member of my own fan club.
I can open up to people who won't reject me.
I'm in good company even when I am alone.
I've been rejected; therefore I am.

23

The Perfect Relationship?

Myth

I should be able to make and keep the perfect relationship.
If it's not perfect, there must be something wrong with one of us.

Truth

There is no perfect relationship. You are imperfect. So are your significant and insignificant others. Any relationship that includes any of you will be imperfect. Be grateful. Imperfect relationships can change, grow, challenge, expand. Perfection is perhaps about a moment, never about a relationship, never about a life.

Sometime during the dawn of civilization, we all got the message that somewhere there is a perfect relationship, and many of us have been searching for it ever since. Storybook fictions, like the one about the pot of gold at the end of the rainbow, have a simple golden glow that messy real life never achieves.

Take Fred Astaire and Ginger Rogers, for instance. They look pretty perfect in all those old movies. They are aristocratic, elegant, unflappable, in sync, in tune, in perfect harmony. They never stop smiling. They don't step on each other's toes or bump into the wall. They never get dropped on the dance floor. They don't even sweat. Their relationship looks perfect because in the movies everything is illusion, and only illusion is forever. Real life is not so choreographed, not so pretty, not so simple, not so perfect.

All real-life relationships will sometimes be happy, exciting, fun, meaningful, supportive, and fulfilling. Sometimes they'll be bumpy, difficult, boring, terrible, messy, and good enough. Any relationship can be placed on a continuum from fully functional to disgustingly dysfunctional, and there's not much fun at the dysfunctional end.

All functional relationships flex and change when the music changes or someone gets stepped on. In good-enough relationships, the team is as important as each member. Partners stay aware of each other and are able to negotiate who leads and who follows across the dance floor of their lives. They can move apart and come together gracefully, each taking a turn in the spotlight.

People in distressingly dysfunctional relationships are each dancing to different music, going in different directions, making unpredictable moves to an unknown beat. They can't negotiate who leads and who follows. They can't agree when to be together and when to move apart. One is always stepping on the other's toes. One partner may hog the spotlight while the other may refuse to dance at all. The partners may feel joined at the hip and unable to solo. No wonder Fred and Ginger look so good!

In the beginning

Lucy and Desi, Ozzie and Harriet, the Brady Bunch, the Partridge Family, the Donna Reed Show, the Cosbys—TV families provided the role models we grew up with. We carry images of their untroubled relationships into adulthood. We also carry the perfect moments of our own childhoods. From these assorted bits and pieces we create an idealized collage of the forever-perfect relationship based on unattainable, unconditional love.

During the years of our childhood and adolescence, we tasted many kinds of love. We probably had crushes on a third-grade classmate, a sixth-grade teacher, a camp counselor, a Scout leader, a cheerleader, a football player, a basketball coach, an English professor. We worshiped movie stars, rock stars, superheros, and other untouchable idols. Love seemed so near and yet so far. Crushes and puppy loves were ways that we extended our world of caring beyond the family. Over the years we found out more and more about deep feelings, desire, and heartfelt longing. As we got older and more complex, we wanted more reciprocity, more intimacy, more substance, a real dance partner. Dancing in our dreams just wasn't the same as slow dancing with a real live person.

We also found odd notions about perfect relationships buried deep in great grandmother's trunk, with the lavender-scented linens. These tidy, antique models of life and marriage stayed around long after the linens disintegrated. We learned from grandmother that we should be virgins (for girls only) or sexually experienced (for boys only) before we're married. Then we (boys and girls) should be in permanent (until death do us part), monogamous (forsaking all others), heterosexual (bride and groom, man and wife), traditional (lawfully wedded) relationships. If we're not, we've failed, we're flawed, we've broken the rules and violated the natural order of the universe.

But the universe had other ideas. Relationships were and are more difficult and absurd than our grandmothers imagined. Just recently, women couldn't own property because they were property. Recently, people made good matches based solely on financial considerations. Recently, marriages were arranged and had nothing to do with love. Recently, people only lived to be forty, and marriages could easily last forever. Recently, there was no such thing as birth control. Recently, people rarely left the place where they were born, and only married people they'd known all their lives, and there was no divorce, no matter what. Recently, the extended family was the norm. And recently, we realized that the universe was less than perfect then, too.

Because of to unforeseen changes in the world, many of our traditional beliefs are now outdated. Let's reconsider some of the wisdom of the past:

1. Love conquers all.
   False. Love never conquers all.
2. Marriages are made in heaven.
   False. We only say that in retrospect.

3. A good woman is responsible for making a man's life right.
   False. That's not even possible.
4. A good man is responsible for taking perfect care of his woman.
   False. He can't and he doesn't own her.
5. The little woman should be grateful for a roof over her head.
   False. The ungrateful wretch is now taller than she used to be, and an architect.
6. Relationships end because you're not perfect.
   True. They last because you're not perfect, too.
7. Relationships end because your partner is not perfect.
   True. They last because your partner is not perfect, too.
8. Couples must stay together for the sake of the children.
   False. Ask the children.
9. No one ever divorces in our family.
   True. No wonder our family is so unhappy and dysfunctional.
10. You made your bed, now lie in it.
    False. You made your bed, now remake it.
11. Strive for peace at any price.
    False. Peace at any price is too expensive.
12. You're nothing if you're not married.
    False. You're only unmarried if you're not married.
13. You'll be unfulfilled if you don't have children.
    False. You can be fulfilled in ways your grandparents never imagined.

In the present

Good relationships are possible. Perfect relationships are impossible. We all bring our own personal successes, failures, memories, and dreams to every new connection. We learned the art of imperfect relationships from our families, our favorite movies and novels, TV shows and ads, and our previous partners. Every magazine at the checkout stand tells us how to do it, and how to do it better. Just when we think we're beginning to get it right, the relationship changes—a child comes; someone gets sick, goes back to school, or graduates; someone gets laid off; someone gets old or dependent—and everything shifts.

The Perfect Relationship?

Also, about every ten years, the culture's view of relationships changes, evolves, and takes everyone by surprise. The fifties roles, expectations, and partnerships look nothing like the nineties version. Today, we rarely meet future mates at church socials, at band practice, or at our cousin's birthday party. (There are hardly any church socials, most of us aren't in the high school band, and we've never met our cousins, who live in Alaska.) The awkward search for connection happens, nowadays, in bars, gyms, malls, at work, through dating services, the Internet, and personal ads. It's amazing that any two people ever come together at the right time, in the right place, and figure out how to maintain an ongoing, satisfying, good-enough relationship.

Meeting people has never been more difficult. We're all moving so fast, we no longer have casual interactions with the guy who jockeys gas; we self-serve. We don't talk with the bank teller; we use our ATM cards. We don't chat with the grocer; there is no grocer. We touch-tone codes to machines instead of talking to real people on the phone. Sociability is a dying art. We use voice mail, faxes, and e-mail, and rarely hear or see a living, breathing person.

Although our worlds are in some ways expanding, our ability to create intimacy is shrinking. Nowadays it's hard to learn empathy or relate easily to people who are different from ourselves. We've become so isolated that we feel shy most of the time, anticipate rejection, and avoid it by rejecting others first. It's all become so complicated and scary that for many people, the safest connection in the nineties is on the Internet: "It's a perfect relationship. I can't see you. You can't see me. . . . " No wonder we're so reluctant to end any established relationship, no matter how terrible it is. Living, breathing relationships are becoming an endangered species.

When we do meet a new flesh-and-blood person in living color, it's such an enormously important event that we freeze, like a rabbit caught in the headlights. We feel untrained, unskilled in making contact, awkward making small talk or easy conversation. Because the rules are always changing, new meetings seem monumental. We don't know who opens, holds, or closes the door, who drives, who pays, who asks, who leads, who follows, who does, who doesn't, who's tested negative in the last three months. Uncertainty makes every encounter feel risky. And every new friendship feels like a miracle. "Maybe this time I've finally found the perfect relationship. Maybe this new person is really my one true love," and maybe, just maybe, that's so.

At these times, we don't want any reality testing. We want to savor the perfect moments that come with any promising new involvement. All too soon, as we spend time and deepen our knowing, we find that, like life, like us, our new partner is less than perfect. Not wanting to accept this shocking information, we can choose to remain unrealistic and set out to make perfection happen. We can take a perfectly good imperfect relationship and make it a perfectly dysfunctional relationship.

Here are four surefire, fail-safe formulas for disaster that are guaranteed to ruin any relationship.

1. Blame other people for not being perfect. Be cruel. Be sarcastic. Scrutinize and criticize when they least expect it, especially late at night, early in the morning, or when they're sick. Convince them that all problems are their fault. Keep a list of as many problems as possible. Pile them up. Exaggerate them. Never forget, forgive, or let go. Hold grudges. Get even. Reject compromise. Take no responsibility. Repeat often: "If it weren't for you this would be a perfect relationship."

2. Blame yourself for not being perfect. Personalize everything. Scrutinize and criticize yourself. Focus on your shortcomings. Pile them up. Exaggerate them. Never forget them. Never forgive yourself or let go. Convince yourself that all problems are your fault. Reject compromise. Take full responsibility for all mistakes, for not being a perfect mindreader, for not being able to foretell the future. Repeat often: "If it weren't for me, this would be a perfect relationship."

3. Be entirely unrealistic. Pay no attention to history, yours or theirs. Rush into commitments. Repeat the same patterns and believe that this time it will be different. Ignore all real limitations. Expect more than is humanly possible. Blackmail your partner into becoming the perfect parent you never had and giving you all the unconditional love you wanted in childhood.

4. Scatter these killer phrases liberally over your relationships and watch them wither and die:

> If you really loved me, you'd never expect anything from me.
> If you really loved me, you'd never leave me, even for an
> afternoon.
> If you really loved me, you'd never spend any time with
> anyone else.

The Perfect Relationship?

If you really loved me, you'd fight my battles for me.

If you really loved me, you'd change yourself and only do things my way.

If you really loved me, you'd think and feel exactly as I do. We would be as one and never need any boundaries or separateness.

If you really loved me, you'd know what I like, what I want, what I mean, what I don't mean. You'd be able to read my mind. I wouldn't have to talk. My silence would be loud enough for you.

If you really loved me, we'd never argue or disagree about money, work, politics, religion, movies, jokes, decorating, vacations, child rearing, or sex.

If you really loved me, our passion would never fade or need to be renewed.

If you really loved me, you wouldn't survive without me.

If you really loved me, our relationship would be perfect.

Goal

Forget perfect. Establish and cherish the good-enough relationship by being a good-enough partner. Talk. Listen. Laugh. Maintain a highly evolved sense of humor. Avoid being disrespectful, inconsiderate, or mean. Don't blame. Don't criticize. Be willing to apologize. Be open to change. Stay clear about what you like, what you want, where you set your limits. Be flexible. Adapt.

Trust and like yourself. Trust and like your partner. Value your differences. Encourage uniqueness and creativity. Be appreciative. Don't try to overhaul your partner's personality. Be positive. Negotiate the small stuff. Avoid letting it grow into big stuff. Be willing to give. Be willing to receive.

Take responsibility for yourself, your feelings, your behaviors. Let others take responsibility for theirs. Take time to be together. Balance teamwork with separateness, togetherness with solitude. Find a partner who's willing to be good enough, too.

Identify and let go of the bad-enough relationship. Nourishing relationships do not include lies, deceit, cheating, excessive jealousy, threats, name-calling, or physical abuse.

Bad relationships make you feel awful about yourself, your feelings, your values, and your beliefs. Early warning signs include uncontrollable rages, excessive drinking or drugging, big differences in your approaches to work and money. Beware of anyone who abuses children, pets, or property. Avoid anyone who lies to you, puts you down, treats you like a sex object, disappears when you get sick, encourages you to reject your friends and family, puts you in dangerous situations. Be willing to name what's happening. Don't lie to yourself or anyone else. Get a third (and fourth) party to look at the situation. Get help. Get smart. Get out.

Stretch yourself

If you are in a good-enough relationship, enhance it. Recall with pleasure how it began. There were good reasons for getting together in the first place. Remember the good stuff and celebrate it.

Notice what you are and are not willing to change in yourself. Be extra gentle and tender when requesting change in your partner. Chances are your partner will never be very different. Notice how hard it is to change your own behavior. Chances are you will never be very different, either.

Create five positive moments for every negative moment with your partner. Be five times as nice as you are nasty to one another. Offer five compliments for every criticism. This ratio matters.

Work toward shared goals. Support one another's aspirations.

Find the right balance between nourishing the relationship, nourishing yourself, and nourishing your partner. Reevaluate that balance as things change. They will change.

If you are in a bad-enough relationship, find a way to change it or get out. If it feels good, do it. If it doesn't, use your feet.

Make time to be alone. Discover the joys of solitude. Enjoy not being in a significant relationship. Be prepared. All relationships end, except the relationship with yourself.

Affirmations

I can dance in a good-enough relationship.
I know when my relationship isn't working.
I can get help, get smart, get out.
I know when my relationship is good enough.
I'm okay. You're okay. We're okay.
Without you, I am something else.
When I'm alone, I'm in very good company.
I am good enough.
I can allow you and me and this relationship to be imperfect.
I relate; therefore I am.

24

The Flip Side of Perfect

Myth

Perfectionism is not my issue.

Truth

Perfectionism is everyone's issue. We inhale it with the air pollution. We swim in it. Perfectionism grabs us whenever we curse ourselves for being wrong, being late, being dumb. It haunts us when we know we could and should have done better, understood everything, and predicted all the consequences.

In the beginning

We were perfect.

In the present

We're still perfect. We have perfect flaws, bumps, lumps, warts, and two left feet. Perfect, for mere mortals, means falling on our faces on a regular basis, spilling coffee in our laps, making mistakes often and with gusto.

Goal

Allow perfectionism to be your issue, along with control, codependency, romanticism, rejection, guilt, shame, fear, overwork, and gender confusion. You are one of us. Enjoy.

Stretch yourself

Write your own private, favorite perfection myths, the ones that keep you just this side of normal.

Smile knowingly when you encounter anyone's urges to be perfect.

Flaunt being ordinary.

Embrace contradictions.

Question authority.

Affirmations

I love being a perfectionist. I'm in such excellent company.

I love my perfectly ordinary self.

I live in Kansas, not Oz.

I _____ (fill in the blank); therefore I am.

Imperfection Poll

Survey Questions

Circle as many answers as you like.
You will not be graded on this material.

1. I have a deep fear of flawing . . .
   a. Often
   b. Seldom
   c. On Mondays only
   d. Never

2. My priceless imperfections include:

3. My flaws are bigger and better than yours.   True / False

4. My imperfections make me a perfect human being.
   True / False

5. My imperfections and your imperfections make us a perfect
   pair.   True / False

6. I spend valuable, precious time finding and criticizing the tiniest imperfections.
   a. Often
   b. Seldom
   c. On Mondays only
   d. Never

7. I enjoy the imperfections of others more than my own.
   True / False

8. Your imperfections are
   a. Adorable
   b. Interesting and noteworthy
   c. Tiresome
   d. Alarming
   e. All of the above

9. My imperfections are
   a. Adorable
   b. Interesting and noteworthy
   c. Tiresome
   d. Alarming
   e. All of the above

10. My parents made me imperfect
    a. Often
    b. Seldom
    c. On Mondays only
    d. Never

11. My kids make me imperfect
    a. Often
    b. Seldom
    c. On Mondays only
    d. Never